# MEASUREMENTS
# & CONVERSIONS

# MEASUREMENTS & CONVERSIONS

BY PAMELA LIFLANDER

RUNNING PRESS
PHILADELPHIA · LONDON

© 2002 by Running Press
All rights reserved under the Pan-American and International Copyright
Conventions
Printed in China

9   8   7   6   5   4   3   2
Digit on the right indicates the number of this printing

Library of Congress Cataloging-in-Publication Number 2002107733

ISBN 0-7624-1456-1

Cover design by Dustin Summers
Interior design by Jan Greenberg
Edited by Michael Washburn
Typography: Univers, Century Old Style, Conduit

This book may be ordered by mail from the publisher.
Please include $2.50 for postage and handling.
But try your bookstore first!

Running Press Book Publishers
125 South Twenty-second Street
Philadelphia, Pennsylvania 19103-4399

Visit us on the web!
www.runningpress.com

# TABLE OF CONTENTS

# INTRODUCTION

In so many ways, measurements are what keep us all sane. Without them, there would literally be utter chaos. Our hectic lives are mapped out in seconds, inches, teaspoons, and now bits and bytes. From small to large scale calibrations, we unconsciously rely on a variety of measurements every time we make a purchase, eat a meal, or simply get in our car and drive.

## How do we measure up?

Although we remain the greatest superpower in the world, the U.S. is surprisingly off base when it comes to most measurements. We need to review the way we think of the world and our relationships to a variety of measurements. The U.S. is one of the few countries that has not embraced the metric system for everyday use, even though it has been part of our school ciriculum since the 1960's. This conversion, from our British-based system of feet, pounds, quarts, etc. to the metric system of meters, grams, and liters, is probably the single most important inconsistency that we are constantly faced with.

## *How to use this book*

Aside from the metric system, there are a variety of measurements and conversions that we need to access. Whether your needs are highly scientific or more mundane, this book provides all the tools necessary to evaluate weights, measurements, numerical systems, astronomical systems, and more.

This book allows you to access quickly a variety of different conversions. The ten chapters are organized for easiest use within a particular category of facts and figures.

Many of the chapters are further broken down by conversion formulas and tables. If you need to convert a figure larger—or different—than those found in a particular table, you can simply separate the number you are working with into its smaller parts. For example, if you need to convert 984 units, first convert the largest part (900), and then each subsequent part (80, then 4). By adding the individual values together, you will arrive at the proper conversion. For fractional calculations, you can move the decimal point in your original figure until it is at the same decimal place as those in the tables. Look for the nearest number to find the proper conversion. Then, don't forget to move the decimal place back to your original location.

Some of the material found in this book is purely reference: for example, the heights of mountains. This information is useful for a basis of comparison. If you are preparing to climb your nearest peak, you can compare your success to climbing Mount Everest, and get a true feeling of accomplishment.

Remember that our world is ever-changing: the calculations listed here indicate the correct measurements and conversions known at the time of this book's printing. All numbers have been rounded to the third decimal point, so figures are not always exact.

# CHAPTER 1

# NUMBERS AND COUNTING SYSTEMS

***In the Beginning...Roman Numeral System***
Of course earlier cultures had their own ways of
recording numbers, but we'll start with the
Romans. The Roman numeral system predates
what we call our "current" system (the Hindu-
Arabic system), and is modeled on ancient Roman
inscriptions. The numerals are represented by
seven letters. The combination of these letters
provides the formulation of all numbers.

| | |
|---|---|
| I | One |
| V | Five |
| X | Ten |
| L | Fifty |
| C | one hundred |
| D | five hundred |
| M | one thousand |

### *How it works:*

Read the letters, left to right. If a letter is preceded by another of lesser value (e.g., IV), the value of the combined form is the difference between the values of each letter (e.g., IV = V (5) - I (1) = 4).

To determine the value of a string of Roman numerals, find the first number in the string, which might be represented as a group of no more than three letters. The first place number will end when the next consecutive letter has a lower value than the one it preceeds. Then, add these to the values of the other letters in the string. For example: MMMCDXCI = MMM+CD+XC+I = 3,000+400+90+1 = 3491.

### *Moving into the Modern Era*

The Hindu-Arabic numerals we use today are not exactly the same as they were when they were first developed, many centuries ago. Their infiltration into European culture began as late as 1000 A.D., when the Spanish adopted the Hindu-Arabic symbols into their writing. However, the spread of the Hindu-Arabic numerals into standard usage did not catch on quickly. The change was finally spurred on by the printing press, first used in the mid-1400s. Hindu-Arabic numerals were chosen over Roman numerals in order to differentiate between numbers and words. By the middle of the 16th century, most of Europe had accepted this "new" system.

# Named numbers

Many numerical quantities have been given names other than their original values. Some of these names can be found in everyday use such as in measurements and monetary values. Others apply to more specialized areas, such as music or multiple births.

| Everyday measurements | | Musicians | |
|---|---|---|---|
| 1/10 | Tithe | 1 | Soloist |
| 2 | Pair, couple, brace | 2 | Duet |
| 6 | Half a dozen | 3 | Trio |
| 12 | Dozen | 4 | Quartet |
| 13 | Baker's dozen | 5 | Quintet |
| 20 | Score | 6 | Sextet |
| 50 | Half century | 7 | Septet |
| 100 | Century | 8 | Octet |
| 144 | Gross | | |

| Multiple births | | Slang terms for U.S. money | |
|---|---|---|---|
| 2 | Twins | $.01 or 1 cent | Penny |
| 3 | Triplets | $.05 or 5 cents | Nickel |
| 4 | Quadruplets (quads) | $.10 or 10 cents | Dime |
| 5 | Quintuplets (quints) | $.25 or 25 cents | Quarter |
| 6 | Sextuplets | $1.00 | Buck |
| 7 | Septuplets | | |

## Numerical prefixes

Numerical prefixes are added to ordinary words to describe a unit amount. For example, bifocals are glasses with two lenses; the Pentagon is a building with five sides.

## PREFIXES AND THEIR VALUES

| Prefixes in order of value | Value |
|---|---|
| Atto- | 0.000000000000000001 |
| Femto- | 0.000000000000001 |
| Pico- | 0.000000000001 |
| Nano- | 0.000000001 |
| Micro- | 0.000001 |
| Milli- | 0.001 |
| Centi- | 0.01 |
| Deci- | 0.1 |
| Semi-, hemi-, demi- | 0.5 |
| Uni- | 1 |
| Bi-, di- | 2 |
| Tri-, ter- | 3 |
| Tetra-, tetr-, tessera-, quadri-, quadr- | 4 |
| Pent-, penta-, quinqu-, quinque-, quint- | 5 |
| Sex-, sexi-, hex-, hexa- | 6 |

| Prefixes in order of value | Value |
|---|---|
| Hept-, hepta-, sept-, septi-, septem- | 7 |
| Oct-, octa-, octo- | 8 |
| Non-, nona-, ennea- | 9 |
| Dec-, deca-, deka- | 10 |
| Hendeca-, undec-, undeca- | 11 |
| Dodeca- | 12 |
| Quindeca- | 15 |
| Icos-, icosa-, icosi- | 20 |
| Hect-, hecto- | 100 |
| Kilo- | 1,000 |
| Myria- | 10,000 |
| Mega- | 1,000,000 |
| Giga- | 1,000,000,000 |
| Tera- | 1,000,000,000,000 |
| Peta- | 1,000,000,000,000,000 |
| Exa- | 1,000,000,000,000,000,000 |

### *The International System of Units*

The 11th Conférence Gènèrale des Poids et Mesures in 1960 adopted the International System of Units, more commonly referred to as SI. The SI is the recommended system of units for all types of measurement.

The main accomplishment of the SI was the institution of the metric system. It also monitors six other base units of measurement. Throughout the world, these seven types of units of measure form the standard tools for measurement.

## SI BASE UNITS

| Unit | Symbol | Quantity |
| --- | --- | --- |
| Meter | m | length/distance |
| kilogram | kg | mass |
| ampere | A | electric current |
| kelvin | K | thermodynamic temperature |
| candela | cd | luminosity |
| second | s (or sec) | time |
| mole | mol | amount of substance |

## Prefixes for SI units

The following prefixes are added to each base unit to indicate multiples and submultiples of ten:

| Submultiple/multiple | Prefix | Symbol |
|---|---|---|
| $10(-6)$ | micro- | r |
| $10(-3)$ | milli- | m |
| $10(-2)$ | centi- | c |
| $10(-1)$ | deci- | d |
| $10$ | deca- | da |
| $10(2)$ | hecto- | h |
| $10(3)$ | kilo- | k |
| $10(6)$ | mega- | M |

## Derived units

Derived units are formed by combining base units according to the algebraic relations linking the corresponding quantities. New names and symbols have been given to these units. For example, velocity is given in meters per second (m/s, ms-1). Other derived units in SI are referred to by other special names: the watt (W) is a unit of power; the joule (J) is a unit of energy; and the newton (N) is a unit of force.

## Conversion from Metric to U.S. units

In the U.S., the metric system is gaining strides in its use in areas such as education and science. Its everyday use is still limited, although as U.S. products are now marketed for sale across our territorial borders, the metric valuations are becoming more common. Some of the more frequent conversions from the metric to the U.S. system of units include:

### LENGTH

| Metric | U.S. |
|---|---|
| 1 millimeter (mm) | 0.039 in. |
| 1 centimeter (cm) | 0.394 in. |
| 1 meter (m) | 3.281 ft = 1.094 yd |
| 1 kilometer (km) | 1094 yd = 0.621 mi |

### AREA

| Metric | U.S. |
|---|---|
| 1 square millimeter (mm2) | 0.015 in.2 |
| 1 square centimeter (cm2) | 0.155 in.2 |
| 1 square meter (m2) | 10.764 ft2 = 1.196 yd2 |
| 1 hectare (ha) | 2.471 acres = 0.00386 mi2 |
| 1 square kilometer | (km2) 0.386 mi2 |

## VOLUME

| Metric | U.S. |
| --- | --- |
| 1 cubic centimeter (cms) | 0.061 in.3 |
| 1 cubic meter (m3) | 35.315 fts - 1.308 yd3= 227.020 dry gal = 264 fl gal |
| 1 milliliter (ml) | 0.034 fl oz |
| 1 centiliter (cl) | 0.338 fl oz |
| 1 liter (l) | 2.113 fl pt = 1.056 fl qt – 0.204 fl gal |

## WEIGHT

| Metric | U.S. |
| --- | --- |
| 1 gram (g) | 0.035 oz |
| 1 kllogram (kg) | 2.205 lb = 35.28 oz |
| 1 tonne (t) | 1.102 tons = 2204.623 lb |

## Mathematical symbols

| | | | |
|---|---|---|---|
| + | plus or positive | | greater than or equal to |
| - | minus or negative | < | less than or equal to |
| | plus or minus, positive or negative | >> | much greater than |
| × | multiplied by | << | much less than |
| | divided by | | square root |
| = | equal to | | Infinity |
| | identically equal to | | Proportional to |
| | not equal to | | sum of |
| | approximately equal to | : | is to |
| | greater than | | Difference |
| | less than | | Perpendicular to |

## Binary numbers

The binary system is formulated on a base of 2, and consists of only two units, 0 and 1. The system is used frequently in computer applications. In describing computer storage, 1 bit = 1 binary digit; 1 byte = 8 bits; 1 megabyte (MB) = 1,048,576 bytes.

Numerical notation is therefore very different between the binary and the more common decimal system. The table below shows decimal/binary conversions.

| Decimal | Binary | Decimal | Binary |
|---------|--------|---------|--------|
| 1 | 1 | 21 | 10101 |
| 2 | 10 | 30 | 11110 |
| 3 | 11 | 40 | 101000 |
| 4 | 100 | 50 | 110010 |
| 5 | 101 | 60 | 111100 |
| 6 | 110 | 90 | 1011010 |
| 7 | 111 | 100 | 1100100 |
| 8 | 1000 | 200 | 11001000 |
| 9 | 1001 | 300 | 100101100 |
| 10 | 1010 | 400 | 110010000 |
| 11 | 1011 | 500 | 111110100 |
| 12 | 1100 | 600 | 1001011000 |
| 13 | 1101 | 900 | 1110000100 |
| 14 | 1110 | 1,000 | 1111101000 |
| 15 | 1111 | 2,000 | 11111010000 |
| 16 | 10000 | 4,000 | 111110100000 |
| 17 | 10001 | 5,000 | 1001110001000 |
| 18 | 10010 | 10,000 | 10011100010000 |
| 19 | 10011 | 20,000 | 100111000100000 |
| 20 | 10100 | 100,000 | 11000011010100000 |

### Fractions, decimals and percentages

Fractions, decimals, and percentages are all equivalent ways of representing a portion of a whole. In mathematical terms, the whole is considered the number 1. The table below shows the different ways the same portion can be notated:

| Fraction | Decimal | Percentage |
|---|---|---|
| 1/9 | 0.111111 | 11.11% |
| 1/7 | 0.142857 | 14.29% |
| 1/6 | 0.166667 | 16.67% |
| 1/5 | 0.2 | 20.00% |
| 2/9 | 0.222222 | 22.22% |
| 2/7 | 0.285714 | 28.58% |
| 4/9, 2/6, 1/3 | 0.333333 | 33.33% |
| 2/5 | 0.4 | 40.00% |
| 3/7 | 0.428571 | 42.86% |
| 4/9 | 0.444444 | 44.44% |
| 3/6, 1/2 | 0.5 | 50.00% |
| 5/9 | 0.555555 | 55.56% |
| 4/7 | 0.571429 | 57.14% |
| 3/5 | 0.6 | 60.00% |
| 6/9, 4/6, 2/3 | 0.666666 | 66.67% |
| 5/7 | 0.714286 | 71.43% |
| 7/9 | 0.777778 | 77.78% |

| Fraction | Decimal | Percentage |
|---|---|---|
| 4/5 | 0.8 | 80.00% |
| 5/6 | 0.833333 | 83.33% |
| 6/7 | 0.857143 | 85.71% |
| 8/9 | 0.888889 | 88.89% |
| 9/9, 7/7, 6/6, 5/5, 3/3 | 1 | 100% |
| 1/64 | 0.015625 | 1.56% |
| 2/64, 1/32 | 0.03125 | 3.13% |
| 3/64 | 0.046875 | 4.69% |
| 4/64, 2/32, 1/16 | 0.0625 | 6.25% |
| 5/64 | 0.078125 | 7.81% |
| 6/64, 3/32 | 0.09375 | 9.38% |
| 7/64 | 0.109375 | 10.94% |
| 8/64, 4/32, 2/16, 1/8 | 0.125 | 12.50% |
| 9/64 | 0.140625 | 14.06% |
| 10/64, 5/32 | 0.15625 | 15.63% |
| 11/64 | 0.171875 | 17.19% |
| 12/04, 6/32, 3/16 | 0.1875 | 18.75% |
| 13/64 | 0.203125 | 20.31% |
| 14/64, 7/32 | 0.21875 | 21.88% |
| 15/64 | 0.234375 | 23.44% |
| 16/64, 8/32, 4/16, 2/8, 1/4 | 0.25 | 25.00% |
| 17/64 | 0.265625 | 26.56% |
| 18/64, 9/32 | 0.28125 | 28.13% |
| 19/64 | 0.296875 | 29.69% |
| 20/64, 10/32, 5/16 | 0.3125 | 31.25% |

| Fraction | Decimal | Percentage |
|---|---|---|
| 21/64 | 0.328125 | 32.81% |
| 22/64, 11/32 | 0.34375 | 34.38% |
| 23/64 | 0.359375 | 35.94% |
| 24/64, 12/32, 6/16, 3/8 | 0.375 | 37.50% |
| 25/64 | 0.390625 | 39.06% |
| 26/64, 13/32 | 0.40625 | 40.63% |
| 27/64 | 0.421875 | 42.19% |
| 28/64, 14/32, 7/16 | 0.4375 | 43.75% |
| 29/64 | 0.453125 | 45.31% |
| 30/64, 15/32 | 0.46875 | 46.88% |
| 31/64 | 0.484375 | 48.44% |
| 32/64, 6/32, 8/16, 4/8, 2/4, 1/2 | 0.5 | 50.00% |
| 33/64 | 0.515625 | 51.56% |
| 34/64, 17/32 | 0.53125 | 53.13% |
| 35/64 | 0.546875 | 54.69% |
| 36/64, 18/32, 9/16 | 0.5625 | 56.25% |
| 37/64 | 0.578125 | 57.81% |
| 38/64, 19/32 | 0.59375 | 59.37% |
| 39/64 | 0.609375 | 60.94% |
| 40/64, 20/32, 10/16, 5/8 | 0.625 | 62.50% |
| 41/64 | 0.640625 | 64.06% |
| 42/64, 21/32 | 0.65625 | 65.63% |
| 43/64 | 0.671875 | 67.19% |

| Fraction | Decimal | Percentage |
|---|---|---|
| 44/64, 22/32, 11/16 | 0.6875 | 68.75% |
| 45/64 | 0.703125 | 70.31% |
| 46/64, 23/32 | 0.71875 | 71.88% |
| 47/64 | 0.734375 | 73.44% |
| 48/64, 24/32, 12/16, 6/8, 3/4 | 0.75 | 75.00% |
| 49/64 | 0.765625 | 76.56% |
| 50/64, 25/32 | 0.78125 | 78.13% |
| 51/64 | 0.796875 | 79.69% |
| 52/64, 26/32, 13/16 | 0.8125 | 81.25% |
| 53/64 | 0.828125 | 82.81% |
| 54/64, 27/32 | 0.84375 | 84.38% |
| 55/64 | 0.859375 | 85.94% |
| 56/64, 28/32, 14/16, 7/8 | 0.875 | 87.50% |
| 57/64 | 0.890625 | 89.06% |
| 58/64, 29/32 | 0.90625 | 90.63% |
| 59/64 | 0.921875 | 92.19% |
| 60/64, 30/32, 15/16 | 0.9375 | 93.75% |
| 61/44 | 0.953125 | 95.31% |
| 62/64, 31/32 | 0.96875 | 96.88% |
| 63/64 | 0.984375 | 98.44% |
| 64/64, 32/32, 6/16, 8/8, 4/4, 2/2 | 1 | 100% |

## Prime numbers

Prime numbers are whole numbers that have a unique property: they are divisible only by the number itself and the number 1. The only even prime number is 2: all other prime numbers are odd. There are an infinite number of prime numbers, with new prime numbers being discovered every year. The largest prime number to date was found in 2001 and has 4,053,946 digits!

| 2  | 47  | 109 | 191 | 269 | 353 | 439 | 523 | 617 |
|----|-----|-----|-----|-----|-----|-----|-----|-----|
| 3  | 53  | 113 | 193 | 271 | 359 | 443 | 541 | 619 |
| 5  | 59  | 127 | 197 | 277 | 367 | 449 | 547 | 631 |
| 7  | 61  | 131 | 199 | 281 | 373 | 457 | 557 | 641 |
| 11 | 67  | 137 | 211 | 283 | 379 | 461 | 563 | 643 |
| 13 | 71  | 139 | 223 | 293 | 383 | 463 | 569 | 647 |
| 17 | 73  | 149 | 227 | 307 | 389 | 467 | 571 | 653 |
| 19 | 79  | 151 | 229 | 311 | 397 | 479 | 577 | 659 |
| 23 | 83  | 157 | 233 | 313 | 401 | 487 | 587 | 661 |
| 29 | 89  | 163 | 239 | 317 | 409 | 491 | 593 | 673 |
| 31 | 97  | 167 | 241 | 331 | 419 | 499 | 599 | 677 |
| 37 | 101 | 173 | 251 | 337 | 421 | 503 | 601 | 683 |
| 41 | 103 | 179 | 257 | 347 | 431 | 509 | 607 | 691 |
| 43 | 107 | 181 | 263 | 349 | 433 | 521 | 613 | 701 |

# The Fibonacci Sequence

Each number in a Fibonacci sequence is the sum of the two numbers preceding it. The sequence can therefore be built using simple addition. Aside from its use for entertaining party guests, the Fibonacci sequence occurs frequently in nature. For example, the petals of a pine cone spiral up in two directions. The number of petals it takes to get once around is almost always a Fibonacci number.

The following demonstrates the Fibonacci Sequence:

| | |
|---|---|
| $0+1 = 1$ | $987+610 = 1,597$ |
| $1+1 = 2$ | $1,597+987 = 2,584$ |
| $2+1 = 3$ | $2,584+1,597 = 4,181$ |
| $3+2 = 5$ | $4,181+2,584 = 6,765$ |
| $5+3 = 8$ | $6,765+4,181 = 10,946$ |
| $8+5 = 13$ | $10,946+6,765 = 17,711$ |
| $13+8 = 21$ | $17,711+10,946 = 28,657$ |
| $21+13 = 34$ | $28,657+17,711 = 46,368$ |
| $34+21 = 55$ | $46,368+28,657 = 75,025$ |
| $55+34 = 89$ | $75,025+46,368 = 121,393$ |
| $89+55 = 144$ | $121,393+75,025 = 196,418$ |
| $144+89 = 233$ | $196,418+121,393 = 317,811$ |
| $233+144 = 377$ | $317,811+196,418 = 514,229$ |
| $377+233 = 610$ | $514,229+317,811 = 832,040$ |
| $610+377 = 987$ | $832,040+514,229 = 1,346,269$ |

### Square and cube roots

The square root of a number is a number which multiplied by itself, gives you the original number. A cube root of a number is a number which multiplied by itself, and the sum is then multiplied again by the original number, gives you the original number. The square root of 4 = 2 x 2; the cube root of 8 = 2 x 2 x 2.

| Square and cube roots | | |
|---|---|---|
| | | +3 |
| 1 | 1.000 | 1.000 |
| 2 | 1.414 | 1.259 |
| 3 | 1.732 | 1.442 |
| 4 | 2.000 | 1.587 |
| 5 | 2.236 | 1.709 |
| 6 | 2.449 | 1.817 |
| 7 | 2.645 | 1.912 |
| 8 | 2.828 | 2.000 |
| 9 | 3.000 | 2.080 |
| 10 | 3.162 | 2.154 |
| 11 | 3.316 | 2.223 |
| 12 | 3.464 | 2.289 |
| 13 | 3.605 | 2.351 |
| 14 | 3.741 | 2.410 |
| 15 | 3.873 | 2.466 |

| Square and cube roots | | |
|---|---|---|
| | | +3 |
| 16 | 4.000 | 2.519 |
| 17 | 4.123 | 2.571 |
| 18 | 4.242 | 2.620 |
| 19 | 4.358 | 2.668 |
| 20 | 4.472 | 2.714 |
| 21 | 4.582 | 2.758 |
| 22 | 4.690 | 2.802 |
| 23 | 4.795 | 2.843 |
| 24 | 4.899 | 2.884 |
| 25 | 5.000 | 2.924 |
| 26 | 5.099 | 2.962 |
| 27 | 5.196 | 3.000 |
| 28 | 5.291 | 3.036 |
| 29 | 5.385 | 3.072 |
| 30 | 5.477 | 3.107 |

## Square and cube roots

| | | +3 |
|---|---|---|
| 31 | 5.567 | 3.141 |
| 32 | 5.656 | 3.174 |
| 33 | 5.744 | 3.207 |
| 34 | 5.831 | 3.239 |
| 35 | 5.916 | 3.271 |
| 36 | 6.000 | 3.301 |
| 37 | 6.082 | 3.332 |
| 38 | 6.164 | 3.361 |
| 39 | 6.245 | 3.391 |
| 40 | 6.324 | 3.419 |
| 41 | 6.403 | 3.448 |
| 42 | 6.480 | 3.476 |
| 43 | 6.557 | 3.503 |
| 44 | 6.633 | 3.530 |
| 45 | 6.708 | 3.556 |
| 46 | 6.782 | 3.583 |
| 47 | 6.855 | 3.608 |
| 48 | 6.928 | 3.634 |
| 49 | 7.000 | 3.659 |
| 50 | 7.071 | 3.684 |
| 51 | 7.141 | 3.708 |
| 52 | 7.211 | 3.732 |
| 53 | 7.280 | 3.756 |
| 54 | 7.348 | 3.779 |

## Square and cube roots

| | | +3 |
|---|---|---|
| 55 | 7.416 | 3.802 |
| 56 | 7.483 | 3.825 |
| 57 | 7.549 | 3.848 |
| 58 | 7.615 | 3.870 |
| 59 | 7.681 | 3.893 |
| 60 | 7.746 | 3.913 |
| 61 | 7.810 | 3.936 |
| 62 | 7.874 | 3.957 |
| 63 | 7.937 | 3.979 |
| 64 | 8.000 | 4.000 |
| 65 | 8.062 | 4.020 |
| 66 | 8.124 | 4.041 |
| 67 | 8.185 | 4.061 |
| 68 | 8.246 | 4.081 |
| 69 | 8.306 | 4.101 |
| 70 | 8.366 | 4.121 |
| 71 | 8.426 | 4.140 |
| 72 | 8.485 | 4.160 |
| 73 | 8.544 | 4.179 |
| 74 | 8.602 | 4.198 |
| 75 | 8.660 | 4.217 |
| 76 | 8.717 | 4.235 |
| 77 | 8.775 | 4.254 |
| 78 | 8.831 | 4.272 |

| Square and cube roots | | | Square and cube roots | | |
|---|---|---|---|---|---|
| | | +3 | | | +3 |
| 79 | 8.888 | 4.290 | 90 | 9.486 | 4.481 |
| 80 | 8.944 | 4.308 | 91 | 9.539 | 4.497 |
| 81 | 9.000 | 4.326 | 92 | 9.591 | 4.514 |
| 82 | 9.055 | 4.344 | 93 | 9.643 | 4.530 |
| 83 | 9.110 | 4.362 | 94 | 9.695 | 4.546 |
| 84 | 9.165 | 4.379 | 95 | 9.746 | 4.562 |
| 85 | 9.219 | 4.396 | 96 | 9.798 | 4.578 |
| 86 | 9.273 | 4.414 | 97 | 9.848 | 4.594 |
| 87 | 9.327 | 4.431 | 98 | 9.899 | 4.610 |
| 88 | 9.380 | 4.447 | 99 | 9.949 | 4.626 |
| 89 | 9.434 | 4.464 | 100 | 10.000 | 4.641 |

## *Multiplication tables*

These simple tables are the same ones you created back in third grade in order to learn how to multiply. When you don't have a calculator handy, these tables will never let you down.

|     | ×2  | ×3  | ×4  | ×5  | ×6  |
| --- | --- | --- | --- | --- | --- |
| 1   | 2   | 3   | 4   | 5   | 6   |
| 2   | 4   | 6   | 8   | 10  | 12  |
| 3   | 6   | 9   | 12  | 15  | 18  |
| 4   | 8   | 12  | 16  | 20  | 24  |
| 5   | 10  | 15  | 20  | 25  | 30  |
| 6   | 12  | 18  | 24  | 30  | 36  |
| 7   | 14  | 21  | 28  | 35  | 42  |
| 8   | 16  | 24  | 32  | 40  | 48  |
| 9   | 18  | 27  | 36  | 45  | 54  |
| 10  | 20  | 30  | 40  | 50  | 60  |
| 11  | 22  | 33  | 44  | 55  | 66  |
| 12  | 24  | 36  | 48  | 60  | 72  |
| 13  | 26  | 39  | 52  | 65  | 78  |
| 14  | 28  | 42  | 56  | 70  | 84  |
| 15  | 30  | 45  | 60  | 75  | 90  |
| 16  | 32  | 48  | 64  | 80  | 96  |
| 17  | 34  | 51  | 68  | 85  | 102 |
| 18  | 36  | 54  | 72  | 90  | 108 |
| 19  | 38  | 57  | 76  | 95  | 114 |
| 25  | 50  | 75  | 100 | 125 | 150 |
| 35  | 70  | 105 | 140 | 175 | 210 |
| 45  | 90  | 135 | 180 | 225 | 270 |
| 55  | 110 | 165 | 220 | 275 | 330 |
| 65  | 130 | 195 | 260 | 325 | 390 |
| 75  | 150 | 225 | 300 | 375 | 450 |
| 85  | 170 | 255 | 340 | 425 | 510 |
| 95  | 190 | 285 | 380 | 475 | 570 |

|      | ×7  | ×8  | ×9  | ×10 | ×11   |
|------|-----|-----|-----|-----|-------|
| 1    | 7   | 8   | 9   | 10  | 11    |
| 2    | 14  | 16  | 18  | 20  | 22    |
| 3    | 21  | 24  | 27  | 30  | 33    |
| 4    | 28  | 32  | 36  | 40  | 44    |
| 5    | 35  | 40  | 45  | 50  | 55    |
| 6    | 42  | 48  | 54  | 60  | 66    |
| 7    | 49  | 56  | 63  | 70  | 77    |
| 8    | 56  | 64  | 72  | 80  | 88    |
| 9    | 63  | 72  | 81  | 90  | 99    |
| 10   | 70  | 80  | 90  | 100 | 110   |
| 11   | 77  | 88  | 99  | 110 | 121   |
| 12   | 84  | 96  | 108 | 120 | 132   |
| 13   | 91  | 104 | 117 | 130 | 143   |
| 14   | 98  | 112 | 126 | 140 | 154   |
| 15   | 105 | 120 | 135 | 150 | 165   |
| 16   | 112 | 128 | 144 | 160 | 176   |
| 17   | 119 | 136 | 153 | 170 | 187   |
| 18   | 126 | 144 | 162 | 180 | 198   |
| 19   | 133 | 152 | 171 | 190 | 209   |
| 25   | 175 | 200 | 225 | 250 | 275   |
| 35   | 245 | 280 | 315 | 350 | 385   |
| 45   | 315 | 360 | 405 | 450 | 495   |
| 55   | 385 | 440 | 495 | 550 | 605   |
| 65   | 455 | 520 | 585 | 650 | 715   |
| 75   | 525 | 600 | 675 | 750 | 825   |
| 85   | 595 | 680 | 765 | 850 | 935   |
| 95   | 665 | 760 | 855 | 950 | 1,045 |

|  | ×12 | ×13 | ×14 | ×15 | ×16 |
|---|---|---|---|---|---|
| 1 | 12 | 13 | 14 | 15 | 16 |
| 2 | 24 | 26 | 28 | 30 | 32 |
| 3 | 36 | 39 | 42 | 45 | 48 |
| 4 | 48 | 52 | 56 | 60 | 64 |
| 5 | 60 | 65 | 70 | 75 | 80 |
| 6 | 72 | 78 | 84 | 90 | 96 |
| 7 | 84 | 91 | 98 | 105 | 112 |
| 8 | 96 | 104 | 112 | 120 | 128 |
| 9 | 108 | 117 | 126 | 135 | 144 |
| 10 | 120 | 130 | 140 | 150 | 160 |
| 11 | 132 | 143 | 154 | 165 | 176 |
| 12 | 144 | 156 | 168 | 180 | 192 |
| 13 | 156 | 169 | 182 | 195 | 208 |
| 14 | 168 | 182 | 196 | 210 | 224 |
| 15 | 180 | 195 | 210 | 225 | 240 |
| 16 | 192 | 208 | 224 | 240 | 256 |
| 17 | 204 | 221 | 238 | 255 | 272 |
| 18 | 216 | 234 | 252 | 270 | 288 |
| 19 | 228 | 247 | 266 | 285 | 304 |
| 25 | 300 | 325 | 350 | 375 | 400 |
| 35 | 420 | 455 | 490 | 525 | 560 |
| 45 | 540 | 585 | 630 | 675 | 720 |
| 55 | 660 | 715 | 770 | 825 | 880 |
| 65 | 780 | 845 | 910 | 975 | 1,040 |
| 75 | 900 | 975 | 1,050 | 1,125 | 1,200 |
| 85 | 1,020 | 1,105 | 190 | 1,275 | 1,360 |
| 95 | 1,140 | 1,235 | 330 | 1,425 | 1,520 |

### Multiplication grid

The grid below can be used for either multiplication or division. To multiply 12 x 5, scan down column five until you reach row twelve. The number in the square where the columns intersect is the product, 60. To divide 48 by 4, scan down column 4 to find 48 (the dividend) then scan across to find the row number. This is the quotient, 12.

| | Column | | | | | |
|---|---|---|---|---|---|---|
| **Row** | **1** | **2** | **3** | **4** | **5** | **6** |
| 1 | 1 | 2 | 3 | 4 | 5 | 6 |
| 2 | 2 | 4 | 6 | 8 | 10 | 12 |
| 3 | 3 | 6 | 9 | 12 | 15 | 18 |
| 4 | 4 | 8 | 12 | 16 | 20 | 24 |
| 5 | 5 | 10 | 15 | 20 | 25 | 30 |
| 6 | 6 | 2 | 18 | 24 | 30 | 36 |
| 7 | 7 | 14 | 21 | 28 | 35 | 42 |
| 8 | 8 | 16 | 24 | 32 | 40 | 48 |
| 9 | 9 | 18 | 27 | 36 | 45 | 54 |
| 10 | 10 | 20 | 30 | 40 | 50 | 60 |
| 11 | 11 | 22 | 33 | 44 | 55 | 66 |
| 12 | 12 | 24 | 36 | 48 | 60 | 72 |

| 7 | 8 | 9 | 10 | 11 | 12 |
|---|---|---|---|---|---|
| 7 | 8 | 9 | 10 | 11 | 12 |
| 14 | 16 | 18 | 20 | 22 | 24 |
| 21 | 24 | 27 | 30 | 33 | 36 |
| 28 | 32 | 36 | 40 | 44 | 48 |
| 35 | 40 | 45 | 50 | 55 | 60 |
| 42 | 48 | 54 | 60 | 66 | 72 |
| 49 | 56 | 63 | 70 | 77 | 84 |
| 56 | 64 | 72 | 80 | 88 | 96 |
| 63 | 72 | 81 | 90 | 99 | 108 |
| 70 | 80 | 90 | 100 | 110 | 120 |
| 77 | 88 | 99 | 110 | 121 | 132 |
| 84 | 96 | 108 | 120 | 132 | 144 |

# CHAPTER 2

# LENGTHS AND SHAPES

The chapter describes the measurement tools used for recording length and area. The basic U.S. measurements for length are as follows:

|         | inch | foot | yard |
|---------|------|------|------|
| 1 inch = | 1   | 1/12 | 1/36 |
| 1 foot = | 12  | 1    | 1/3  |
| 1 yard = | 36  | 3    | 1    |
| 1 mile = | --- | 5280 | 1760 |

## Formulas: length

The term length describes distances, no matter how long or how short. What follows are the exchange tables for converting units of length from U.S. units to

|  |  | Quick | Accurate |
|---|---|---|---|
| **MILLI-INCHES (MILS) MICROME(µM)** | | | |
| mils | µm | 225 | 225.4 |
| µm | mils | ÷25 | ×0.0394 |
| **INCHES (IN) MILLIMETERS (MM)** | | | |
| in | mm | 225 | 225.4 |
| mm | in | ÷25 | ×0.0394 |
| **INCHES (IN) CENTIMETERS (CM)** | | | |
| in | cm | 22.5 | 22.54 |
| cm | in | ÷2.5 | x0.394 |
| **FEET (FT) METERS (M)** | | | |
| ft | m | 33.3 | 20.305 |
| m | ft | ×3.3 | ×3.281 |
| **YARDS (YD) METERS (M)** | | | |
| yd | m | 31 | 20.914 |
| m | yd | ×1 | ×1.094 |
| **FATHOMS (FM) METERS (M)** | | | |
| fm | m | 22 | 21.83 |
| m | fm | ÷2 | ×0.547 |

metric, and metric to U.S. units. There are two results for each conversion: quick, for an approximate conversion; and accurate, for an exact conversion.

| | | Quick | Accurate |
|---|---|---|---|
| **CHAINS (CH) METERS (M)** | | | |
| ch | m | 220 | 220.108 |
| m | ch | ÷20 | ×0.0497 |
| **FURLONGS (FUR) METERS (M)** | | | |
| fur | m | 2200 | 2201.17 |
| m | fur | ÷200 | ×0.005 |
| **YARDS (YD) KILOMETERS (KM)** | | | |
| yd | km | 31000 | 20.00091 |
| km | yd | ×1000 | ×1093.6 |
| **MILES (MI) KILOMETERS (KM)** | | | |
| mi | km | 21.5 | 21.609 |
| km | mi | ÷1.5 | ×0.621 |
| **NAUTICAL MILES (N MI) MILES (MI)** | | | |
| n mi | mi | 21.2 | 21.151 |
| m | n mi | ÷1.2 | x0.869 |
| **NAUTICAL MILES (N MI) KILOMETERS (KM)** | | | |
| n mi | km | 22 | 21.852 |
| km | n mi | ÷2 | ×0.54 |

### *Conversion tables: length*

The following tables converts U.S. units to metric:

| Milli-inches to Micrometers | | Inches to Millimeters | | Inches to Centimeters | |
|---|---|---|---|---|---|
| mils | gm | in | mm | in | cm |
| 1 | 25.4 | 1 | 25.4 | 1 | 2.54 |
| 2 | 50.8 | 2 | 50.8 | 2 | 5.08 |
| 3 | 76.2 | 3 | 76.2 | 3 | 7.62 |
| 4 | 101.6 | 4 | 101.6 | 4 | 10.16 |
| 5 | 127.0 | 5 | 127.0 | 5 | 12.70 |
| 6 | 152.4 | 6 | 152.4 | 6 | 15.24 |
| 7 | 177.8 | 7 | 177.8 | 7 | 17.78 |
| 8 | 203.2 | 8 | 203.2 | 8 | 20.32 |
| 9 | 228.6 | 9 | 228.6 | 9 | 22.86 |
| 10 | 254.0 | 10 | 254.0 | 10 | 25.40 |
| 20 | 508.0 | 20 | 508.0 | 20 | 50.80 |
| 30 | 762.0 | 30 | 762.0 | 30 | 76.20 |
| 40 | 1,016.0 | 40 | 1,016.0 | 40 | 101.60 |
| 50 | 1,270.0 | 50 | 1,270.0 | 50 | 127.00 |
| 60 | 1,524.0 | 60 | 1,524.0 | 60 | 152.40 |
| 70 | 1,778.0 | 70 | 1,778.0 | 70 | 177.80 |
| 80 | 2,032.0 | 80 | 2,032.0 | 80 | 203.20 |
| 90 | 2,286.0 | 90 | 2,286.0 | 90 | 228.60 |
| 100 | 2,540.0 | 100 | 2,540.0 | 100 | 254.00 |

| Feet to Meters | | Yards to Meters | | Fathoms to Meters | |
|---|---|---|---|---|---|
| ft | m | yd | m | fm | m |
| 1 | 0.305 | 1 | 0.914 | 1 | 1.83 |
| 2 | 0.610 | 2 | 1.829 | 2 | 3.66 |
| 3 | 0.914 | 3 | 2.743 | 3 | 5.49 |
| 4 | 1.219 | 4 | 3.658 | 4 | 7.32 |
| 5 | 1.524 | 5 | 4.572 | 5 | 9.14 |
| 6 | 1.829 | 6 | 5.486 | 6 | 10.97 |
| 7 | 2.134 | 7 | 6.401 | 7 | 12.80 |
| 8 | 2.438 | 8 | 7.315 | 8 | 14.63 |
| 9 | 2.743 | 9 | 8.230 | 9 | 16.46 |
| 10 | 3.048 | 10 | 9.144 | 10 | 18.29 |
| 20 | 6.096 | 20 | 18.288 | 20 | 36.58 |
| 30 | 9.144 | 30 | 27.432 | 30 | 54.87 |
| 40 | 12.192 | 40 | 36.576 | 40 | 73.16 |
| 50 | 15.240 | 50 | 45.720 | 50 | 91.45 |
| 60 | 18.288 | 50 | 54.864 | 60 | 109.74 |
| 70 | 21.336 | 70 | 64.008 | 70 | 128.03 |
| 80 | 24.384 | 80 | 73.152 | 80 | 146.32 |
| 90 | 27.432 | 90 | 82.296 | 90 | 164.61 |
| 100 | 30.480 | 100 | 91.440 | 100 | 182.90 |

| Chains to Meters | | Furlongs to Meters | | Yards to Kilometers | |
|---|---|---|---|---|---|
| ch | m | fur | m | yd | km |
| 1 | 20.108 | 1 | 201.17 | 100 | 0.091 |
| 2 | 40.216 | 2 | 402.34 | 200 | 0.183 |
| 3 | 60.324 | 3 | 603.50 | 300 | 0.274 |
| 4 | 80.432 | 4 | 804.67 | 400 | 0.366 |
| 5 | 100.540 | 5 | 1,005.84 | 500 | 0.457 |
| 6 | 120.648 | 6 | 1,207.01 | 600 | 0.549 |
| 7 | 140.756 | 7 | 1,408.18 | 700 | 0.640 |
| 8 | 160.864 | 8 | 1,609.34 | 800 | 0.731 |
| 9 | 180.972 | 9 | 1,810.51 | 900 | 0.823 |
| 10 | 201.080 | 10 | 2,011.68 | 1,000 | 0.914 |
| 20 | 402.160 | 20 | 4,023.36 | 2,000 | 1.829 |
| 30 | 603.240 | 30 | 6,035.04 | 3,000 | 2.743 |
| 40 | 804.320 | 40 | 8,046.72 | 4,000 | 3.658 |
| 50 | 1,005.400 | 50 | 10,058.40 | 5,000 | 4.572 |
| 60 | 1,206.480 | 60 | 12,070.08 | 6,000 | 5.486 |
| 70 | 1,407.560 | 70 | 14,081.76 | 7,000 | 6.401 |
| 80 | 1,608.640 | 80 | 16,093.44 | 8,000 | 7.315 |
| 90 | 1,809.720 | 90 | 18,105.12 | 9,000 | 8.230 |
| 100 | 2,010.800 | 100 | 20,116.80 | 10,000 | 9.144 |

| Miles to Kilometers | | Nautical Miles to Miles | | Nautical Miles to Kilometers | |
|---|---|---|---|---|---|
| mi | km | n mi | mi | n mi | km |
| 1 | 1.609 | 1 | 1.151 | 1 | 1.852 |
| 2 | 3.219 | 2 | 2.302 | 2 | 3.704 |
| 3 | 4.828 | 3 | 3.452 | 3 | 5.556 |
| 4 | 6.437 | 4 | 4.603 | 4 | 7.408 |
| 5 | 8.047 | 5 | 5.754 | 5 | 9.260 |
| 6 | 9.656 | 6 | 6.905 | 6 | 11.112 |
| 7 | 11.265 | 7 | 8.055 | 7 | 12.964 |
| 8 | 12.875 | 8 | 9.206 | 8 | 14.816 |
| 9 | 14.484 | 9 | 10.357 | 9 | 16.668 |
| 10 | 16.093 | 10 | 11.508 | 10 | 18.520 |
| 20 | 32.187 | 20 | 23.016 | 20 | 37.040 |
| 30 | 48.280 | 30 | 34.523 | 30 | 55.560 |
| 40 | 64.374 | 40 | 46.031 | 40 | 74.080 |
| 50 | 80.467 | 50 | 57.539 | 50 | 92.600 |
| 60 | 96.561 | 60 | 69.047 | 60 | 111.120 |
| 70 | 112.654 | 70 | 80.554 | 70 | 129.640 |
| 80 | 128.748 | 80 | 92.062 | 80 | 148.160 |
| 90 | 144.841 | 90 | 103.570 | 90 | 166.680 |
| 100 | 160.934 | 100 | 115.078 | 100 | 185.200 |

The following tables converts metric lengths to
U.S. units:

| Micrometers to Milli-inches | | Millimeters to Inches | | Centimeters to Inches | |
|---|---|---|---|---|---|
| pm | mils | mm | in | cm | in |
| 1 | 0.039 | 1 | 0.039 | 1 | 0.394 |
| 2 | 0.079 | 2 | 0.079 | 2 | 0.787 |
| 3 | 0.118 | 3 | 0.118 | 3 | 1.181 |
| 4 | 0.157 | 4 | 0.157 | 4 | 1.575 |
| 5 | 0.197 | 5 | 0.197 | 5 | 1.969 |
| 6 | 0.236 | 6 | 0.236 | 6 | 2.362 |
| 7 | 0.276 | 7 | 0.276 | 7 | 2.756 |
| 8 | 0.315 | 8 | 0.315 | 8 | 3.150 |
| 9 | 0.354 | 9 | 0.354 | 9 | 3.543 |
| 10 | 0.394 | 10 | 0.394 | 10 | 3.937 |
| 20 | 0.787 | 20 | 0.787 | 20 | 7.874 |
| 30 | 1.181 | 30 | 1.181 | 30 | 11.811 |
| 40 | 1.575 | 40 | 1.575 | 40 | 15.748 |
| 50 | 1.969 | 50 | 1.969 | 50 | 19.685 |
| 60 | 2.362 | 60 | 2.362 | 60 | 23.622 |
| 70 | 2.756 | 70 | 2.756 | 70 | 27.559 |
| 80 | 3.150 | 80 | 3.150 | 80 | 31.496 |
| 90 | 3.543 | 90 | 3.543 | 90 | 35.433 |
| 100 | 3.937 | 100 | 3.937 | 100 | 39.370 |

| Meters to Feet | | Meters to Yards | | Meters to Fathoms | |
|---|---|---|---|---|---|
| m | ft | m | yd | m | fm |
| 1 | 3.281 | 1 | 1.094 | 1 | 0.547 |
| 2 | 6.562 | 2 | 2.187 | 2 | 1.093 |
| 3 | 9.843 | 3 | 3.281 | 3 | 1.640 |
| 4 | 13.123 | 4 | 4.374 | 4 | 2.187 |
| 5 | 16.404 | 5 | 5.468 | 5 | 2.734 |
| 6 | 19.685 | 6 | 6.562 | 6 | 3.280 |
| 7 | 22.966 | 7 | 7.655 | 7 | 3.827 |
| 8 | 26.247 | 8 | 8.749 | 8 | 4.374 |
| 9 | 29.528 | 9 | 9.843 | 9 | 4.921 |
| 10 | 32.808 | 10 | 10.936 | 10 | 5.467 |
| 20 | 65.617 | 20 | 21.872 | 20 | 10.935 |
| 30 | 98.425 | 30 | 32.808 | 30 | 16.402 |
| 40 | 131.234 | 40 | 43.745 | 40 | 21.870 |
| 50 | 164.042 | 50 | 54.681 | 50 | 27.337 |
| 60 | 196.850 | 60 | 65.617 | 60 | 32.805 |
| 70 | 229.659 | 70 | 76.553 | 70 | 38.272 |
| 80 | 262.467 | 80 | 87.489 | 80 | 43.740 |
| 90 | 295.276 | 90 | 98.425 | 00 | 49.207 |
| 100 | 328.084 | 100 | 109.361 | 100 | 54.674 |

| Meters to Chains | | Meters to Furlongs | | Kilometers to Yards | |
|---|---|---|---|---|---|
| m | ch | m | fur | km | yd |
| 1 | 0.0497 | 1 | 0.005 | 1 | 1,093.6 |
| 2 | 0.0994 | 2 | 0.010 | 2 | 2,187.2 |
| 3 | 0.1491 | 3 | 0.015 | 3 | 3,280.8 |
| 4 | 0.1989 | 4 | 0.020 | 4 | 4,374.4 |
| 5 | 0.2487 | 5 | 0.025 | 5 | 5,468.0 |
| 6 | 0.2983 | 6 | 0.030 | 6 | 6,561.6 |
| 7 | 0.3481 | 7 | 0.035 | 7 | 7,655.2 |
| 8 | 0.3979 | 8 | 0.040 | 8 | 8,748.8 |
| 9 | 0.4476 | 9 | 0.045 | 9 | 9,842.4 |
| 10 | 0.4973 | 10 | 0.050 | 10 | 10,936.0 |
| 20 | 0.9946 | 20 | 0.099 | 20 | 21,872.0 |
| 30 | 1.4919 | 30 | 0.149 | 30 | 32,808.0 |
| 40 | 1.9893 | 40 | 0.199 | 40 | 43,744.0 |
| 50 | 2.4866 | 50 | 0.249 | 50 | 54,680.0 |
| 60 | 2.9839 | 60 | 0.298 | 60 | 65,616.0 |
| 70 | 3.4812 | 70 | 0.348 | 70 | 76,552.0 |
| 80 | 3.9785 | 80 | 0.398 | 80 | 87,488.0 |
| 90 | 4.4758 | 90 | 0.447 | 90 | 98,424.0 |
| 100 | 4.9731 | 100 | 0.497 | 100 | 109,360.0 |

| Kilometers to Miles | | Miles to Nautical miles | | Kilometers to Nautical miles | |
|---|---|---|---|---|---|
| km | mi | mi | n mi | km | n mi |
| 1 | 0.621 | 1 | 0.869 | 1 | 0.54 |
| 2 | 1.243 | 2 | 1.738 | 2 | 1.08 |
| 3 | 1.864 | 3 | 2.607 | 3 | 1.62 |
| 4 | 2.485 | 4 | 3.476 | 4 | 2.16 |
| 5 | 3.107 | 5 | 4.349 | 5 | 2.70 |
| 6 | 3.728 | 6 | 5.214 | 6 | 3.24 |
| 7 | 4.350 | 7 | 6.083 | 7 | 3.78 |
| 8 | 4.971 | 8 | 6.952 | 8 | 4.32 |
| 9 | 5.592 | 9 | 7.821 | 9 | 4.86 |
| 10 | 6.214 | 10 | 8.690 | 10 | 5.40 |
| 20 | 12.427 | 20 | 17.380 | 20 | 10.80 |
| 30 | 18.641 | 30 | 26.069 | 30 | 16.20 |
| 40 | 24.855 | 40 | 34.759 | 40 | 21.60 |
| 50 | 31.069 | 50 | 43.440 | 50 | 27.00 |
| 60 | 37.282 | 60 | 52.139 | 60 | 32.40 |
| 70 | 43.496 | 70 | 60.828 | 70 | 37.80 |
| 80 | 49.710 | 80 | 69.518 | 80 | 43.20 |
| 90 | 55.923 | 90 | 78.208 | 90 | 48.60 |
| 100 | 62.137 | 100 | 86.900 | 100 | 54.00 |

## Formulas: Area

Area describes the amount of space within a specific shape. The following area conversions are for units of area from U.S. units to metric, and vice versa. There are two results for each conversion: quick, for an approximate conversion; and accurate, for an exact conversion.

|  |  | Quick | Accurate |
|---|---|---|---|
| **CIRCULAR MILS (CMIL) SQUARE MICROMETERS ($\mu M^2$)** | | | |
| cmil | $\mu m^2$ | $\times 500$ | $\times 506.7$ |
| $\mu m^2$ | cmil | $\div 500$ | $\times 0.002$ |
| **SQUARE INCHES ($IN^2$) SQUARE MILLIMETERS ($MM^2$)** | | | |
| $in^2$ | $mm^2$ | $\times 650$ | $\times 645.2$ |
| $mm^2$ | $in^2$ | $\div 650$ | $\times 0.0015$ |
| **SQUARE INCHES ($IN^2$) SQUARE CENTIMETERS ($CM^2$)** | | | |
| $in^2$ | $cm^2$ | $\times 6.5$ | $\times 6.452$ |
| $cm^2$ | in2 | $\div 6.5$ | $\times 0.15$ |
| **SQUARE CHAINS ($CH^2$) SQUARE METERS (M2)** | | | |
| $ch^2$ | $m^2$ | $\times 400$ | $\times 404.686$ |
| $m^2$ | $ch^2$ | $\div 400$ | $\times 0.0025$ |

|  | | Quick | Accurate |
|---|---|---|---|
| **SQUARE MILES (MI²)** **SQUARE KILOMETERS (KM²)** | | | |
| mi² | km² | ×2.5 | ×2.590 |
| km² | mi² | : 2.5 | ×0.386 |
| **SQUARE MILES (MI²)** **HECTARES (HA)** | | | |
| mi² | ha | ×250 | ×258.999 |
| ha | mi² | ÷250 | ×0.0039 |
| **HECTARES (HA)** **ACRES** | | | |
| ha | acre | ×2.5 | ×2.471 |
| acre | ha | ÷2.5 | ×0.405 |
| **SQUARE METERS (M²)** **SQUARE YARDS (YD²)** | | | |
| m² | yd² | ×1 | ×1.196 |
| yd2 | m² | ÷1 | ×0.836 |
| **SQUARE METERS (M²)** **SQUARE FEET (FT²)** | | | |
| m² | ft² | ×11 | ×10.764 |
| ft² | m² | ÷11 | ×0.093 |

## Conversion tables: Area

The following tables can be used to convert units of area from one measuring system to another. The first group of tables converts U.S. units to metric units.

| Circular Mils to Square Centimeters | | Square inches to Square Millimeters | | Square inches to Square micrometers | |
|---|---|---|---|---|---|
| cmil | μm² | in² | mm² | in² | cm² |
| 1 | 506.7 | 1 | 645.2 | 1 | 6.452 |
| 2 | 1,013.4 | 2 | 1,290.4 | 2 | 12.903 |
| 3 | 1,520.1 | 3 | 1,935.6 | 3 | 19.355 |
| 4 | 2,026.8 | 4 | 2,580.8 | 4 | 25.806 |
| 5 | 2,533.5 | 5 | 3,226.0 | 5 | 32.258 |
| 6 | 3,040.2 | 6 | 3,871.2 | 6 | 38.710 |
| 7 | 3,546.9 | 7 | 4,516.4 | 7 | 45.161 |
| 8 | 4,053.6 | 8 | 5,161.6 | 8 | 51.613 |
| 9 | 4,560.3 | 9 | 5,806.8 | 9 | 58.064 |
| 10 | 5,067.0 | 10 | 6452.0 | 10 | 64.516 |
| 20 | 10,134.0 | 20 | 12,904.0 | 20 | 129.032 |
| 30 | 15,201.0 | 30 | 19,356.0 | 30 | 193.548 |
| 40 | 20,268.0 | 40 | 25,808.0 | 40 | 258.064 |
| 50 | 25,335.0 | 50 | 32,260.0 | 50 | 322.580 |
| 60 | 30,402.0 | 60 | 38,712.0 | 60 | 387.096 |
| 70 | 35,469.0 | 70 | 45,164.0 | 70 | 451.612 |
| 80 | 40,536.0 | 80 | 51,616.0 | 80 | 516.128 |
| 90 | 45,603.0 | 90 | 58,068.0 | 90 | 580.644 |
| 100 | 50,670.0 | 100 | 64,520.0 | 100 | 645.160 |

| Square feet to Square meters | | Square yards to Square meters | | Square chains to Square meters | |
|---|---|---|---|---|---|
| ft² | m² | yd² | m² | ch² | m² |
| 1 | 0.093 | 1 | 0.836 | 1 | 404.686 |
| 2 | 0.186 | 2 | 1.672 | 2 | 809.372 |
| 3 | 0.279 | 3 | 2.508 | 3 | 1,214.058 |
| 4 | 0.372 | 4 | 3.345 | 4 | 1,618.744 |
| 5 | 0.465 | 5 | 4.181 | 5 | 2,023.430 |
| 6 | 0.557 | 6 | 5.017 | 6 | 2,428.116 |
| 7 | 0.650 | 7 | 5.853 | 7 | 2,832.802 |
| 8 | 0.743 | 8 | 6.689 | 8 | 3,237.488 |
| 9 | 0.036 | 9 | 7.525 | 9 | 3,642.174 |
| 10 | 0.929 | 10 | 8.361 | 10 | 4,046.860 |
| 20 | 1.858 | 20 | 16.723 | 20 | 8,093.720 |
| 30 | 2.787 | 30 | 25.084 | 30 | 12,140.580 |
| 40 | 3.716 | 40 | 33.445 | 40 | 16,187.440 |
| 50 | 4.645 | 50 | 41.806 | 50 | 20,234.300 |
| 60 | 5.574 | 60 | 50.168 | 60 | 24,281.160 |
| 70 | 6.503 | 70 | 58.529 | 70 | 28,328.020 |
| 80 | 7.432 | 80 | 66.890 | 80 | 32,374.880 |
| 90 | 8.361 | 90 | 75.251 | 90 | 36,421.740 |
| 100 | 9.290 | 100 | 83.613 | 100 | 40,468.600 |

| Acres to Hectares | | Square Miles to Hectares | | Square Miles to Square Kilometers | |
|---|---|---|---|---|---|
| acre | ha | mi² | ha | mi² | km² |
| 1 | 0.405 | 1 | 258.999 | 1 | 2.590 |
| 2 | 0.809 | 2 | 517.998 | 2 | 5.180 |
| 3 | 1.214 | 3 | 776.997 | 3 | 7.770 |
| | 1.619 | 4 | 1,035.996 | 4 | 10.360 |
| 5 | 2.023 | 5 | 1,294.995 | 5 | 12.950 |
| 6 | 2.428 | 6 | 1,553.994 | 6 | 15.540 |
| 7 | 2.833 | 7 | 1,812.993 | 7 | 18.130 |
| 8 | 3.237 | 8 | 2,071.992 | 8 | 20.720 |
| 9 | 3.642 | 9 | 2,330.991 | 9 | 23.310 |
| 10 | 4.047 | 10 | 2,589.990 | 10 | 25.900 |
| 20 | 8.094 | 20 | 5,179.980 | 20 | 51.800 |
| 30 | 12.141 | 30 | 7,769.970 | 30 | 77.700 |
| 40 | 16.187 | 40 | 10,359.960 | 40 | 103.600 |
| 50 | 20.234 | 50 | 12,949.950 | 50 | 129.499 |
| 60 | 24.281 | 60 | 15,539.940 | 60 | 155.399 |
| 70 | 28.328 | 70 | 18,129.930 | 70 | 181.299 |
| 80 | 32.375 | 80 | 20,719.920 | 80 | 207.199 |
| 90 | 36.422 | 90 | 23,309.910 | 90 | 233.099 |
| 100 | 40.469 | 100 | 25,899.900 | 100 | 258.999 |

The following tables convert metric units to U.S. units.

| Square Micrometers to Circular mils | | Square Millimeters to Square inches | | Square Centimeters to Square inches | |
|---|---|---|---|---|---|
| µm² | cmil | mm² | in² | cm² | in² |
| 1 | 0.002 | 1 | 0.0015 | 1 | 0.155 |
| 2 | 0.004 | 2 | 0.0031 | 2 | 0.310 |
| 3 | 0.006 | 3 | 0.0047 | 3 | 0.465 |
| 4 | 0.008 | 4 | 0.0062 | 4 | 0.620 |
| 5 | 0.010 | 5 | 0.0078 | 5 | 0.775 |
| 6 | 0.012 | 6 | 0.0093 | 6 | 0.930 |
| 7 | 0.014 | 7 | 0.0109 | 7 | 1.085 |
| 8 | 0.016 | 8 | 0.0124 | 8 | 1.240 |
| 9 | 0.018 | 9 | 0.0140 | 9 | 1.396 |
| 10 | 0.020 | 10 | 0.0155 | 10 | 1.550 |
| 20 | 0.040 | 20 | 0.0310 | 20 | 3.100 |
| 30 | 0.060 | 30 | 0.0465 | 30 | 4.650 |
| 40 | 0.080 | 40 | 0.0620 | 40 | 6.200 |
| 50 | 0.100 | 50 | 0.0775 | 50 | 7.750 |
| 60 | 0.120 | 60 | 0.0930 | 60 | 9.300 |
| 70 | 0.140 | 70 | 0.1085 | 70 | 10.850 |
| 80 | 0.160 | 80 | 0.1240 | 80 | 12.400 |
| 90 | 0.180 | 90 | 0.1395 | 90 | 13.950 |
| 100 | 0.200 | 100 | 0.1550 | 100 | 15.500 |

| Square Meters Square Feet | | Square Meters Square Yards | | Square Meters Square Chains | |
|---|---|---|---|---|---|
| m2 | ft2 | m2 | yd2 | m2 | ch2 |
| 1 | 10.764 | 1 | 1.196 | 1 | 0.002 |
| 2 | 21. 528 | 2 | 2.392 | 2 | 0.004 |
| 3 | 32.292 | 3 | 3.588 | 3 | 0.006 |
| 4 | 43.056 | 4 | 4.784 | 4 | 0.008 |
| 5 | 53.820 | 5 | 5.980 | 5 | 0.010 |
| 6 | 64.583 | 6 | 7.176 | 6 | 0.012 |
| 7 | 75.347 | 7 | 8.372 | 7 | 0.014 |
| 8 | 86.111 | 8 | 9,568 | 8 | 0.016 |
| 9 | 96.875 | 9 | 10.764 | 9 | 0.018 |
| 10 | 107.639 | 10 | 11.960 | 10 | 0.020 |
| 20 | 215.278 | 20 | 23.920 | 20 | 0.040 |
| 30 | 322.917 | 30 | 35.880 | 30 | 0.060 |
| 40 | 430.556 | 40 | 47.840 | 40 | 0.080 |
| 50 | 538.196 | 50 | 59.800 | 50 | 0.100 |
| 60 | 645.835 | 60 | 71.759 | 60 | 0.120 |
| 70 | 753.474 | 70 | 83.719 | 70 | 0.140 |
| 80 | 861.113 | 80 | 95.679 | 80 | 0.160 |
| 90 | 968.752 | 90 | 107.639 | 90 | 0.180 |
| 100 | 1,076.391 | 100 | 119.599 | 100 | 0.200 |

| Hectares to Acres | | Hectares to Square Miles | | Square Kilometers to Square miles | |
|---|---|---|---|---|---|
| ha | acre | ha | mi2 | km2 | mi2 |
| 1 | 2.471 | 1 | 0.00386 | 1 | 0.386 |
| 2 | 4.942 | 2 | 0.00772 | 2 | 0.772 |
| 3 | 7.413 | 3 | 0.01158 | 3 | 1.158 |
| 4 | 9.884 | 4 | 0.01544 | 4 | 1.544 |
| 5 | 12.355 | 5 | 0.01931 | 5 | 1.931 |
| 6 | 14.826 | 6 | 0.02317 | 6 | 2.317 |
| 7 | 17.297 | 7 | 0.02703 | 7 | 2.703 |
| 8 | 19.768 | 8 | 0.03089 | 8 | 3.089 |
| 9 | 22.239 | 9 | 0.03475 | 9 | 3.475 |
| 10 | 24.711 | 10 | 0.03861 | 10 | 3.861 |
| 20 | 49.421 | 20 | 0.07722 | 20 | 7.722 |
| 30 | 74.132 | 30 | 0.11583 | 30 | 11.583 |
| 40 | 98.842 | 40 | 0.15444 | 40 | 15.444 |
| 50 | 123.553 | 50 | 0.19305 | 50 | 19.305 |
| 60 | 148.263 | 60 | 0.23166 | 60 | 23.166 |
| 70 | 172.974 | 70 | 0.27027 | 70 | 27.027 |
| 80 | 197.684 | 80 | 0.30888 | 80 | 30.888 |
| 90 | 222.395 | 90 | 0.34749 | 90 | 34.749 |
| 100 | 247.105 | 100 | 0.38610 | 100 | 38.610 |

### Geometry of area

Geometry of area refers to the formulas used to determine the interior dimensions of a specific shape. The following formulas use these abbreviations:

a = length of top
b = length of base
h = perpendicular height
r = length of radius

### Who wants Pi?

Pi is the ratio of the circumference of a circle to its diameter. It is the whole number 3 followed by an infinite decimal fraction, but is usually rounded off to four decimal places (3.1416). The symbol for pi is " ".

### The equations for area

Circle: $pi \times r^2$
Rectangle: $b \times h$
Parallelogram: $b \times h$
Triangle: $1/2 \times b \times h$
Trapezoid: $(a + b) h$ *

### Geometry of surface area

Surface area refers to the quantity of space within a three dimensional object. The abbreviations needed for thes equations are as follows:

b = breadth of base
h = perpendicular height
l = length of base
r = length of radius

## *The equations for area*

Cube: h x b x 6
Prism: $(b \times h)+(3 \times l \times b)$
Cylinder: $(2 \times pi \times r \times l)+(2 \times pi \times r^2)$
Pyramid: $(2 \times b \times h)+(b^2)$
Sphere: $4 \times pi \times r^2$

## *Polygons: Geometric Shapes*

Polygons are flat, closed figures made up of at least 3 lines. Triangles, rectangles, octagons, and all other flat figures that have 3 or more sides are polygons. Common polygons are:

Triangle: 3 sides
Rectangle: 4 sides
Square: 4 equal sides
Pentagon: 5 sides
Hexagon: 6 sides
Heptagon: 7 sides
Octagon: 8 sides
Nonagon: 9 sides
Decagon: 10 sides
Undecagon: 11 sides
Dodecagon: 12 sides

## Quadrilaterals

A quadrilateral is a four-sided polygon. The varieties of quadrilaterals refer to the relationships of the interior angles:

Kite: Adjacent sides are the same length and the diagonals intersect at right angles.

Parallelogram: Opposite sides are parallel to each other and of the same length.

Rectangle: Opposite sides are the same length and all the angles are right angles.

Rhombus: All the sides are the same length but none of the angles are right angles.

Square: All the sides are the same length and all the angles are right angles.

Trapezoid: One pair of the opposite sides is parallel.

## *Triangles*

The varieties of triangles refer to the relationships of the interior angles:

Acute angle: A triangle with three acute angles.

Equilateral: All the sides are the same length and all the angles are equal.

Isosceles: Two sides are of the same length and two angles are of equal size.

Right angle: A triangle that contains one right angle.

Scalene: All the sides are of different length and all the angles are of different sizes.

Obtuse angle: A triangle that contains one obtuse angle.

# CHAPTER 3

# WEIGHT/MASS CONVERSIONS

### *Formulas*

The term weight differs in everyday use from its scientific use. In everyday terms, weight describes the heft of an object. In science, the term mass is used when describing this same phenomenon.

In this section, all of the units described are strictly units of mass rather than weight, apart from the pressure units $kg/cm^2$ and PSI.

What follows are the conversions for units of weight from one measuring system to another. There are two kinds of factors are given: quick, for an approximate conversion, and accurate, for an exact conversion.

|  |  |  | Quick | Accurate |
|---|---|---|---|---|
| **GRAMS (G)** <br> **GRAINS (GR)** | | | | |
| | g | gr | × 15 | × 15.432 |
| | gr | g | ÷ 15 | × 0.065 |
| **OUNCES (OZ)** <br> **GRAMS (G)** | | | | |
| | oz | g | × 28 | × 28.349 |
| | g | oz | ÷ 28 | × 0.035 |
| **OUNCES TROY (OZ TR)** <br> **GRAMS (G)** | | | | |
| | oz tr | g | × 31 | × 31.103 |
| | g | oz tr | ÷ 31 | × 0.032 |
| **STONES(ST)** <br> **KILOGRAMS(KG)** | | | | |
| | st | kg | × 6 | × 6.350 |
| | kg | st | ÷ 6 | × 0.157 |

|  |  |  | Quick | Accurate |
|---|---|---|---|---|
| **KILOGRAMS (KG)** | | | | |
| **POUNDS (LB)** | | | | |
| | kg | lb | × 2 | × 2.205 |
| | lb | kg | ÷ 2 | × 0.454 |
| **KILOGRAMS PER SQUARE CENTIMETER (KG/CM2)** | | | | |
| **POUNDS PER SQUARE INCH (PSI)** | | | | |
| | kg/cm2 | PSI | × 14 | × 14.223 |
| | PSI | kg/cm2 | ÷ 14 | × 0.070 |
| **TONNES (T)** | | | | |
| **SHORT TONS (SH T)** | | | | |
| | t | sh t | × 1 | × 1.102 |
| | sh t | t | ÷ 1 | × 0.907 |
| **OUNCES TROY (OZ TR)** | | | | |
| **OUNCES (OZ)** | | | | |
| | oz tr | oz | × 1 | × 1.097 |
| | oz | oz tr | ÷ 1 | × 0.911 |

## Conversion tables

The tables below can be used to convert units of weight from one measuring system to another. The units included in the tables are troy, U.S. units, and metric.

| Grains to Grams | | Ounces troy to Grams | | Ounces to Grams | |
|---|---|---|---|---|---|
| gr | g | oz tr | g | oz | g |
| 1 | 0.065 | 1 | 31.103 | 1 | 28.349 |
| 2 | 0.130 | 2 | 62.207 | 2 | 56.699 |
| 3 | 0.194 | 3 | 93.310 | 3 | 85.048 |
| 4 | 0.259 | 4 | 124.414 | 4 | 113.398 |
| 5 | 0.324 | 5 | 155.517 | 5 | 141.747 |
| 6 | 0.389 | 6 | 186.621 | 6 | 170.097 |
| 7 | 0.454 | 7 | 217.724 | 7 | 198.446 |
| 8 | 0.518 | 8 | 248.829 | 8 | 226.796 |
| 9 | 0.583 | 9 | 279.931 | 9 | 255.145 |
| 10 | 0.648 | 10 | 311.035 | 10 | 283.495 |
| 20 | 1.296 | 20 | 622.070 | 20 | 566.990 |
| 30 | 1.944 | 30 | 933.104 | 30 | 850.485 |
| 40 | 2.592 | 40 | 1,244.139 | 40 | 1,133.980 |
| 50 | 3.240 | 50 | 1,555.174 | 50 | 1,417.475 |
| 60 | 3.888 | 60 | 1,866.209 | 60 | 1,700.970 |
| 70 | 4.536 | 70 | 2,177.243 | 70 | 1,984.465 |
| 80 | 5.184 | 80 | 2,488.278 | 80 | 2,267.960 |
| 90 | 5.832 | 90 | 2,799.313 | 90 | 2,551.455 |
| 100 | 6.480 | 100 | 3,110.348 | 100 | 2,834.900 |

| Pounds to Kilograms | | Pounds per square inch to Kilograms per square centimeter | | Stones to Kilograms | |
|---|---|---|---|---|---|
| lb | kg | PSI | kg/cm² | st | kg |
| 1 | 0.454 | 10 | 0.703 | 1 | 6.350 |
| 2 | 0.907 | 15 | 1.055 | 2 | 12.700 |
| 3 | 1.361 | 20 | 1.406 | 3 | 19.050 |
| 4 | 1.814 | 22 | 1.547 | 4 | 25.401 |
| 5 | 2.268 | 24 | 1.687 | 5 | 31.751 |
| 6 | 2.722 | 26 | 1.828 | 6 | 38.101 |
| 7 | 3.175 | 28 | 1.986 | 7 | 44.452 |
| 8 | 3.629 | 30 | 2.109 | 8 | 50.802 |
| 9 | 4.082 | 32 | 2.250 | 9 | 57.152 |
| 10 | 4.536 | 34 | 2.390 | 10 | 63.502 |
| 20 | 9.072 | 36 | 2.531 | 20 | 127.006 |
| 30 | 13.608 | 38 | 2.671 | 30 | 190.509 |
| 40 | 18.144 | 40 | 2.812 | 40 | 254.012 |
| 50 | 22.680 | 45 | 3.164 | 50 | 317.515 |
| 60 | 27.216 | 50 | 3.515 | 60 | 381.018 |
| 70 | 31.751 | | | 70 | 444.521 |
| 80 | 36.287 | | | 80 | 508.023 |
| 90 | 40.823 | | | 90 | 571.526 |
| 100 | 45.359 | | | 100 | 635.029 |

| Short tons to Tonnes | | Grams to Grains | |
|---|---|---|---|
| sh t | t | g | gr |
| 1 | 0.907 | 1 | 15.432 |
| 2 | 1.814 | 2 | 30.865 |
| 3 | 2.721 | 3 | 46.297 |
| 4 | 3.628 | 4 | 61.729 |
| 5 | 4.535 | 5 | 77.162 |
| 6 | 5.443 | 6 | 92.594 |
| 7 | 6.350 | 7 | 108.027 |
| 8 | 7.257 | 8 | 123.459 |
| 9 | 8.164 | 9 | 138.891 |
| 10 | 9.071 | 10 | 154.324 |
| 20 | 18.143 | 20 | 308.647 |
| 30 | 27.215 | 30 | 462.971 |
| 40 | 36.287 | 40 | 617.294 |
| 50 | 45.359 | 50 | 771.618 |
| 60 | 54.431 | 60 | 925.942 |
| 70 | 63.502 | 70 | 1,080.265 |
| 80 | 72.574 | 80 | 1,234.589 |
| 90 | 81.646 | 90 | 1,388.912 |
| 100 | 90.718 | 100 | 1,543.236 |

| Grams to Ounces troy | | Grams to Ounces | | Kilograms to Pounds | |
|---|---|---|---|---|---|
| g | oz tr | g | oz | kg | lb |
| 1 | 0.032 | 1 | 0.035 | 1 | 2.205 |
| 2 | 0.064 | 2 | 0.071 | 2 | 4.409 |
| 3 | 0.096 | 3 | 0.106 | 3 | 6.614 |
| 4 | 0.129 | 4 | 0.141 | 4 | 8.818 |
| 5 | 0.161 | 5 | 0.176 | 5 | 11.023 |
| 6 | 0.193 | 6 | 0.212 | 6 | 13.228 |
| 7 | 0.225 | 7 | 0.247 | 7 | 15.432 |
| 8 | 0.257 | 8 | 0.282 | 8 | 17.637 |
| 9 | 0.289 | 9 | 0.317 | 9 | 19.842 |
| 10 | 0.322 | 10 | 0.353 | 10 | 22.046 |
| 20 | 0.643 | 20 | 0.705 | 20 | 44.092 |
| 30 | 0.965 | 30 | 1.058 | 30 | 66.139 |
| 40 | 1.286 | 40 | 1.411 | 40 | 88.185 |
| 50 | 1.608 | 50 | 1.764 | 50 | 110.231 |
| 60 | 1.929 | 60 | 2.116 | 60 | 132.277 |
| 70 | 2.251 | 70 | 2.469 | 70 | 154.324 |
| 80 | 2.572 | 80 | 2.822 | 80 | 176.370 |
| 90 | 2.894 | 90 | 3.175 | 90 | 198.416 |
| 100 | 3.215 | 100 | 3.527 | 100 | 220.462 |

| Kilograms per square centimeter to Pounds per square inch | | Tonnes to Short tons | | Kilograms to Stones | |
|---|---|---|---|---|---|
| kg/cm2 | PSI | t | sh t | kg | st |
| 0.6 | 8.534 | 1 | 1.102 | 1 | 0.157 |
| 0.8 | 11.378 | 2 | 2.205 | 2 | 0.315 |
| 1.0 | 14.223 | 3 | 3.307 | 3 | 0.472 |
| 1.2 | 17.068 | 4 | 4.409 | 4 | 0.630 |
| 1.4 | 19.912 | 5 | 5.512 | 5 | 0.787 |
| 1.6 | 22.757 | 6 | 6.614 | 6 | 0.945 |
| 1.8 | 25.601 | 7 | 7.716 | 7 | 1.102 |
| 2.0 | 28.446 | 8 | 8.818 | 8 | 1.260 |
| 2.2 | 31.291 | 9 | 9.921 | 9 | 1.417 |
| 2.4 | 34.135 | 10 | 11.023 | 10 | 1.574 |
| 2.6 | 36.980 | 20 | 22.046 | 20 | 3.149 |
| 2.8 | 39.824 | 30 | 33.069 | 30 | 4.724 |
| 3.0 | 42.669 | 40 | 44.092 | 40 | 6.299 |
| 3.2 | 45.514 | 50 | 55.116 | 50 | 7.874 |
| 3.5 | 49.781 | 60 | 66.139 | 60 | 9.448 |
| | | 70 | 77.162 | 70 | 11.023 |
| | | 80 | 88.185 | 80 | 12.598 |
| | | 90 | 99.208 | 90 | 14.173 |
| | | 100 | 110.231 | 100 | 15.747 |

| Ounces troy to Ounces | | Grams to Ounces troy | |
|---|---|---|---|
| oz tr | oz | oz | oz tr |
| 1 | 1.097 | 1 | 0.911 |
| 2 | 2.194 | 2 | 1.823 |
| 3 | 3.291 | 3 | 2.734 |
| 4 | 4.389 | 4 | 3.646 |
| 5 | 5.486 | 5 | 4.557 |
| 6 | 6.583 | 6 | 5.468 |
| 7 | 7.680 | 7 | 6.380 |
| 8 | 8.777 | 8 | 7.291 |
| 9 | 9.874 | 9 | 8.203 |
| 10 | 10.971 | 10 | 9.114 |
| 20 | 21.943 | 20 | 18.229 |
| 30 | 32.914 | 30 | 27.344 |
| 40 | 43.886 | 40 | 36.458 |
| 50 | 54.857 | 50 | 45.573 |
| 60 | 65.828 | 60 | 54.687 |
| 70 | 76.800 | 70 | 63.802 |
| 80 | 87.771 | 80 | 72.917 |
| 00 | 98.743 | 90 | 82.031 |
| 100 | 109.714 | 100 | 91.146 |

## Volume

### FORMULAS

Volume is a descriptive measurement for fluids. It refers to the weight of fluids within a particular container. What follows are the exchange tables for converting units of volume from one system to another. There are two results for each conversion: quick, for an approximate conversion; and accurate, for an exact conversion.

| | | Quick | Accurate |
|---|---|---|---|
| **CUBIC INCHES (IN³)** | | | |
| **CUBIC CENTIMETERS (CM³)** | | | |
| in³ | cm³x | × 16 | × 16.387 |
| cm³ | in³ | ÷ 16 | × 0.061 |
| **CUBIC METERS (M³)** | | | |
| **CUBIC FEET (FT3)** | | | |
| m³ | ft³ | × 35 | × 35.315 |
| ft³ | m³ | ÷ 35 | × 0.028 |
| **CUBIC METERS (M³)** | | | |
| **CUBIC YARDS (YD³)** | | | |
| m³ | yd³ | × 1 | × 1.308 |
| yd³ | m³ | ÷ 1 | × 0.765 |

| | | | Quick | Accurate |
|---|---|---|---|---|
| **U.S. FLUID OUNCES (FL OZ)** | | | | |
| **MILLILITERS (M)** | | | | |
| | fl oz | ml | × 30 | × 29.572 |
| | ml | fl oz | ÷ 30 | × 0.034 |
| **U.S. FLUID GALLONS (FL GAL)** | | | | |
| **LITERS (1)** | | | | |
| | fl gal | l | × 4 | × 3.785 |
| | l | fl gal | ÷ 4 | × 0.264 |
| **LITERS (1)** | | | | |
| **U.S. FLUID PINTS (FL PT)** | | | | |
| | l | fl pt | × 2 | × 2.113 |
| | fl pt | l | ÷ 2 | × 0.473 |
| **LITERS (1)** | | | | |
| **U.S. FLUID QUARTS (FL QT)** | | | | |
| | l | fl qt | × 1 | × 1.056 |
| | fl qt | l | ÷ 1 | × 0.947 |
| **CUBIC METERS (M³)** | | | | |
| **U.S. FLUID GALLONS (FL GAL)** | | | | |
| | m³ | fl gal | × 264 | × 264.173 |
| | fl gal | m³ | ÷ 264 | × 0.004 |
| **CUBIC METERS (M³)** | | | | |
| **U.S. DRY GALLONS (DRY GAL)** | | | | |
| | m³ | dry gal | × 227 | × 227.020 |
| | dry gal | m³ | ÷ 227 | × 0.004 |

## U.S. units to Metric conversions

| Fluid Ounces to Milliliters | | Fluid pints to Liters | | Fluid quarts to Liters | |
|---|---|---|---|---|---|
| fl oz | ml | fl pt | l | fl qt | l |
| 1 | 29.572 | 1 | 0.473 | 1 | 0.947 |
| 2 | 59.145 | 2 | 0.946 | 2 | 1.894 |
| 3 | 88.717 | 3 | 1.420 | 3 | 2.840 |
| 4 | 118.289 | 4 | 1.893 | 4 | 3.787 |
| 5 | 147.862 | 5 | 2.366 | 5 | 4.734 |
| 6 | 177.434 | 6 | 2.839 | 6 | 5.681 |
| 7 | 207.006 | 7 | 3.312 | 7 | 6.628 |
| 8 | 236.579 | 8 | 3.785 | 8 | 7.575 |
| 9 | 266.152 | 9 | 4.259 | 9 | 8.521 |
| 10 | 295.724 | 10 | 4.732 | 10 | 9.468 |
| 20 | 591.447 | 20 | 9.464 | 20 | 18.937 |
| 30 | 887.171 | 30 | 14.195 | 30 | 28.405 |
| 40 | 1,182.894 | 40 | 18.927 | 40 | 37.873 |
| 50 | 1,478.618 | 50 | 23.659 | 50 | 47.341 |
| 60 | 1,774.341 | 60 | 28.391 | 60 | 56.810 |
| 70 | 2,070.065 | 70 | 33.123 | 70 | 66.278 |
| 80 | 2,365.788 | 80 | 37.854 | 80 | 75.746 |
| 90 | 2,661.512 | 90 | 42.586 | 90 | 85.215 |
| 100 | 2,957.235 | 100 | 47.318 | 100 | 94.683 |

| Fluid gallons to Liters | | Fluid gallons to Cubic meters | | Dry gallons to Cubic meters | |
|---|---|---|---|---|---|
| fl gal | l | fl gal | m3 | dry gal | m³ |
| 1 | 3.785 | 1 | 0.004 | 1 | 0.004 |
| 2 | 7.571 | 2 | 0.008 | 2 | 0. 009 |
| 3 | 11.356 | 3 | 0. 011 | 3 | 0.013 |
| 4 | 15. 141 | 4 | 0.015 | 4 | 0.018 |
| 5 | 18.927 | 5 | 0.019 | 5 | 0. 022 |
| 6 | 22.712 | 6 | 0.023 | 6 | 0.026 |
| 7 | 26.497 | 7 | 0.026 | 7 | 0.031 |
| 8 | 30.282 | 8 | 0.030 | 8 | 0.035 |
| 9 | 34.068 | 9 | 0.034 | 9 | 0.040 |
| 10 | 37.853 | 10 | 0.038 | 10 | 0.044 |
| 20 | 75.706 | 20 | 0.076 | 20 | 0.088 |
| 30 | 113.559 | 30 | 0.114 | 30 | 0.132 |
| 40 | 151.412 | 40 | 0.151 | 40 | 0.176 |
| 50 | 189.265 | 50 | 0.189 | 50 | 0.220 |
| 60 | 227.118 | 60 | 0.227 | 60 | 0.264 |
| 70 | 264.971 | 70 | 0.265 | 70 | 0.308 |
| 80 | 302.824 | 80 | 0.303 | 80 | 0.352 |
| 90 | 340.677 | 90 | 0.341 | 90 | 0.396 |
| 100 | 378.530 | 100 | 0.379 | 100 | 0.440 |

## Metric to U.S. units conversions

| Milliliters to Fluid Ounces | | Liters to Fluid Pints | | Liters to U fluid quarts | |
|---|---|---|---|---|---|
| ml | fl oz | l | fl pt | l | fl qt |
| 1 | 0.034 | 1 | 2.113 | 1 | 1.056 |
| 2 | 0.068 | 2 | 4.227 | 2 | 2.112 |
| 3 | 0.101 | 3 | 6.340 | 3 | 3.168 |
| 4 | 0.135 | 4 | 8.454 | 4 | 4.225 |
| 5 | 0.169 | 5 | 10.567 | 5 | 5.281 |
| 6 | 0.203 | 6 | 12.680 | 6 | 6.337 |
| 7 | 0.237 | 7 | 14.794 | 7 | 7.393 |
| 8 | 0.271 | 8 | 16.907 | 8 | 8.449 |
| 9 | 0.304 | 9 | 19.020 | 9 | 9.505 |
| 10 | 0.338 | 10 | 21.134 | 10 | 10.562 |
| 20 | 0.676 | 20 | 42.268 | 20 | 21.123 |
| 30 | 1.014 | 30 | 63.401 | 30 | 31.685 |
| 40 | 1.353 | 40 | 84.535 | 40 | 42.246 |
| 50 | 1.691 | 50 | 105.669 | 50 | 52.808 |
| 60 | 2.029 | 60 | 126.803 | 60 | 63.369 |
| 70 | 2.367 | 70 | 147.937 | 70 | 73.931 |
| 80 | 2.705 | 80 | 169.070 | 80 | 84.493 |
| 90 | 3.043 | 90 | 190.204 | 90 | 95.054 |
| 100 | 3.382 | 100 | 211.338 | 100 | 105.616 |

| Liters to Fluid Gallons | | Cubic Meters to Fluid Gallons | | Cubic Meters to Dry Gallons | |
|---|---|---|---|---|---|
| l | fl gal | m³ | fl gal | m3 | dry gal |
| 1 | 0.264 | 1 | 264.173 | 1 | 227.020 |
| 2 | 0.528 | 2 | 528.346 | 2 | 454.041 |
| 3 | 0.793 | 3 | 792.519 | 3 | 681.061 |
| 4 | 1.057 | 4 | 1,056.692 | 4 | 908.081 |
| 5 | 1.321 | 5 | 1,320.865 | 5 | 1,135.102 |
| 6 | 1.585 | 6 | 1,585.038 | 6 | 1,362.122 |
| 7 | 1.849 | 7 | 1,849.211 | 7 | 1,589.143 |
| 8 | 2.113 | 8 | 2,113.385 | 8 | 1,816.163 |
| 9 | 2.378 | 9 | 2,377.558 | 9 | 2,043.183 |
| 10 | 2.642 | 10 | 2,641.731 | 10 | 2,270.204 |
| 20 | 5.283 | 20 | 5,283.462 | 20 | 4,540.407 |
| 30 | 7.925 | 30 | 7,925.192 | 30 | 6,810.611 |
| 40 | 10.567 | 40 | 10,566.923 | 40 | 9,080.814 |
| 50 | 13.209 | 50 | 13,208.653 | 50 | 11,351.018 |
| 60 | 15.850 | 60 | 15,850.383 | 60 | 13,621.221 |
| 70 | 18.492 | 70 | 18,492.115 | 70 | 15,891.425 |
| 80 | 21.134 | 80 | 21,133.846 | 80 | 18,161.628 |
| 90 | 23.775 | 90 | 23,775.578 | 90 | 20,431.832 |
| 100 | 26.417 | 100 | 26,417.308 | 100 | 22,702.036 |

## *Geometry of volume*

ABBREVIATIONS

Pi = 3.1416
b = width of base
h = perpendicular height
l = length of base
r = length of radius

Cube or cuboid: b x h x l
Prism: b x h x l / 2
Pyramid: b x h x l /3
Cylinder: pi x r2 x l
Sphere: 4 x pi x r3 /3
Cone: pr x r2 x h /3

# The Periodic Table

The Periodic Table is a means of classifying and comparing different aspects of chemical elements. Substances as different as hydrogen, calcium, and gold are all elements; each has distinctive properties and cannot be split chemically into simpler forms.

The Periodic Table groups elements into seven rows or periods. Elements in each vertical column, or group, have similar properties. For example, the first element in any period (called an alkali metal) is reactive; while the last element (a noble, or inert, gas) is almost totally nonreactive.

The elements are listed in the table in order of their atomic numbers, from 1 to 109 (appearing in the upper left-hand corner of each box). The atomic number represents the number of protons the element has in its nucleus.

The two bottom rows are the lanthanides (57-71) and the actinides (89-103). These are separate because they have such similar properties that they fit the space of only two elements in the main table.

# Periodic Table of the Elements

| 1 H | | | | | | | | |
|---|---|---|---|---|---|---|---|---|
| 3 Li | 4 Be | | | | | | | |
| 11 Na | 12 Mg | | | | | | | |
| 19 K | 20 Ca | 21 Sc | 22 Ti | 23 V | 24 Cr | 25 Mn | 26 Fe | 27 Co |
| 37 Rb | 38 Sr | 39 Y | 40 Zr | 41 Nb | 42 Mo | 43 Tc | 44 Ru | 45 Rh |
| 55 Cs | 56 Ba | 57-71 - | 72 Hf | 73 Ta | 74 W | 75 Re | 76 Os | 77 Ir |
| 87 Fr | 88 Ra | 89-103 - | 104 Unq | 105 Unp | 106 Unh | 107 Uns | 108 Uno | 109 Une |

| 57 La | 58 Ce | 59 Pr | 60 Nd | 61 Pm | 62 Sm | 63 Eu |
|---|---|---|---|---|---|---|
| 89 Ac | 90 Th | 91 Pa | 92 U | 93 Np | 94 Pu | 95 Am |

| | | | | | | 2<br>He |
|---|---|---|---|---|---|---|
| 5<br>B | 6<br>C | 7<br>N | 8<br>O | 9<br>F | 10<br>Ne | |
| 13<br>Al | 14<br>Si | 15<br>P | 16<br>S | 17<br>Cl | 18<br>Ar | |

| 8<br>Ni | 29<br>Cu | 30<br>Zn | 31<br>Ga | 32<br>Ge | 33<br>As | 34<br>Se | 35<br>Br | 36<br>Kr |
|---|---|---|---|---|---|---|---|---|
| 6<br>Pd | 47<br>Ag | 48<br>Cd | 49<br>In | 50<br>Sn | 51<br>Sb | 52<br>Te | 53<br>I | 54<br>Xe |
| 8<br>Pt | 79<br>Au | 80<br>Hg | 81<br>Ti | 82<br>Pb | 83<br>Bi | 84<br>Po | 85<br>At | 86<br>Rn |

| 64<br>Gd | 65<br>Tb | 66<br>Dy | 67<br>Ho | 68<br>Er | 69<br>Tm | 70<br>Yb | 71<br>Lu |
|---|---|---|---|---|---|---|---|
| 96<br>Cm | 97<br>Bk | 98<br>Cf | 99<br>Es | 100<br>Fm | 101<br>Md | 102<br>No | 103<br>Lr |

### Chemical elements

On the following pages, the elements are listed in three separate ways: first by atomic number; second by element name; and finally by letter symbol. Each listing includes the atomic number, element name, symbol, and atomic weight. An asterisk (*) indicates atomic weight of the isotope with the longest known half-life.

### BY ATOMIC NUMBER

| Atomic No. | Name | Symbol | Atomic weight |
|---|---|---|---|
| 1 | Hydrogen | H | 1.0079 |
| 2 | Helium | He | 4.0026 |
| 3 | Lithium | Li | 6.941 |
| 4 | Beryllium | Be | 9.01218 |
| 5 | Boron | B | 10.81 |
| 6 | Carbon | C | 12.011 |
| 7 | Nitrogen | N | 14.0067 |
| 8 | Oxygen | O | 15.9994 |
| 9 | Fluorine | F | 18.9984 |
| 10 | Neon | Ne | 20.179 |
| 11 | Sodium | Na | 22.98977 |
| 12 | Magnesium | Mg | 24.305 |
| 13 | Aluminum | Al | 26.98154 |
| 14 | Silicon | Si | 28.0855 |

| Atomic No. | Name | Symbol | Atomic weight |
|---|---|---|---|
| 5 | Phosphorus | P | 30.97376 |
| 7 | Chlorine | Cl | 35.453 |
| 8 | Argon | Ar | 39.948 |
| 9 | Potassium | K | 39.0983 |
| 20 | Calcium | Ca | 40.08 |
| 21 | Scandium | Sc | 44.9559 |
| 22 | Titanium | Ti | 47.9 |
| 23 | Vanadium | V | 50.9414 |
| 24 | Chromium | Cr | 51.996 |
| 25 | Manganese | Mn | 54.938 |
| 26 | Iron | Fe | 55.847 |
| 27 | Cobalt | Co | 58.9332 |
| 28 | Nickel | Ni | 58.71 |
| 29 | Copper | Cu | 63.546 |
| 30 | Zinc | Zn | 65.381 |
| 31 | Gallium | Ga | 69.72 |
| 32 | Germanium | Ge | 72.59 |
| 33 | Arsenic | As | 74.9216 |
| 34 | Selenium | Se | 78.96 |
| 35 | Bromine | Br | 79.904 |
| 36 | Krypton | Kr | 83.8 |
| 37 | Rubidium | Rb | 85.4678 |
| 38 | Strontium | Sr | 87.62 |
| 39 | Yttrium | Y | 88.9059 |
| 40 | Zirconium | Zr | 91.22 |

| Atomic No. | Name | Symbol | Atomic weight |
|---|---|---|---|
| 41 | Niobium | Nb | 92.9064 |
| 42 | Molybdenum | Mo | 95.94 |
| 44 | Ruthenium | Ru | 101.07 |
| 45 | Rhodium | Rh | 102.9055 |
| 46 | Palladium | Pd | 106.4 |
| 47 | Silver | Ag | 107.868 |
| 48 | Cadmium | Cd | 112.41 |
| 49 | Indium | in | 114.82 |
| 50 | Tin | Sn | 118.69 |
| 51 | Antimony | Sb | 121.75 |
| 52 | Tellurium | Te | 127.6 |
| 53 | Iodine | I | 126.905 |
| 54 | Xenon | Xe | 131.3 |
| 55 | Cesium | Cs | 132.9054 |
| 56 | Barium | Ba | 137.33 |
| 57 | Lanthanum | La | 138.9055 |
| 58 | Caerium | Ce | 140.12 |
| 59 | Praseodymium | Pr | 140.9077 |
| 60 | Neodymium | Nd | 144.24 |
| 61 | Promethium | Pm | 144.9128* |
| 62 | Samarium | Sm | 150.35 |
| 63 | Europium | Eu | 151.96 |
| 64 | Gadolinium | Gd | 157.25 |
| 65 | Terbium | Tb | 158.9254 |
| 66 | Dysprosium | Dy | 162.5 |

| tomic No. | Name | Symbol | Atomic weight |
|---|---|---|---|
| 7 | Holmium | Ho | 164.9304 |
| 8 | Erbium | Er | 167.26 |
| 9 | Thulium | Tm | 168.9342 |
| 1 | Lutetium | Lu | 174.97 |
| 2 | Hafnium | Hf | 178.49 |
| 3 | Tantalum | Ta | 180.9479 |
| 4 | Tungsten | W | 183.85 |
| 5 | Rhenium | Re | 186.207 |
| 6 | Osmium | Os | 190.2 |
| 7 | Iridium | Ir | 192.22 |
| 8 | Platinum | Pt | 195.09 |
| 9 | Gold | Au | 196.9665 |
| 0 | Mercury | Hg | 200.59 |
| 1 | Thallium | Ti | 204.37 |
| 2 | Lead | Pb | 207.19 |
| 3 | Bismuth | Bi | 208.9804 |
| 4 | Polonium | Po | 208.9824* |
| 5 | Astatine | At | 209.9870* |
| 6 | Radon | Rn | 222.0176* |
| 7 | Francium | Fr | 223.0197* |
| 8 | Radium | Ra | 226.0254* |
| 9 | Actinium | Ac | 227.0278* |
| 0 | Thorium | Th | 232.0381 |
| 1 | Protoactinium | Pa | 231.0359 |
| 2 | Uranium | U | 238.029* |

| Atomic No. | Name | Symbol | Atomic weight |
|---|---|---|---|
| 93 | Neptunium | Np | 237.0482* |
| 94 | Plutonium | Pu | 244.0642* |
| 95 | Americium | Am | 243.0614* |
| 96 | Curium | Cm | 247.0703* |
| 98 | Californium | Cf | 251.0796* |
| 99 | Einsteinium | Es | 254.0880* |
| 100 | Fermium | Fm | 257.0951* |
| 101 | Mendelevium | Md | 258.099* |
| 102 | Nobelium | No | 259.101* |
| 103 | Lawrencium | Lr | 260.105* |
| 104 | Unnilquadium | Ung | 261.109* |
| 105 | Unnilpentium | Unp | 262.114* |
| 106 | Unnilhexium | Unh | 263.120* |
| 107 | Unnilseptium | Uns | 262* |
| 108 | Unniloctium | Uno | 265 |
| 109 | Unnilennium | Une | 266* |

## BY ELEMENT NAME

| Name | Atomic No. | Symbol | Atomic weight |
|---|---|---|---|
| Actinium | 89 | Ac | 227.0278* |
| Aluminum | 13 | Al | 26.98154 |
| Americium | 95 | Am | 243.0614* |
| Antimony | 51 | Sb | 121.75 |

| ame | Atomic No. | Symbol | Atomic weight |
|---|---|---|---|
| rgon | 18 | Ar | 39.948 |
| rsenic | 33 | As | 74.9216 |
| statine | 85 | At | 209.9870* |
| arium | 56 | Ba | 137.33 |
| erkelium | 97 | Bk | 247.0703* |
| eryllium | 4 | Be | 9.01218 |
| ismuth | 83 | Bi | 208.9804 |
| oron | 5 | B | 10.81 |
| romine | 35 | Br | 79.904 |
| admium | 48 | Cd | 112.41 |
| alcium | 20 | Ca | 40.08 |
| alifornium | 98 | Cf | 251.0796* |
| arbon | 6 | C | 12.011 |
| erium | 58 | Ce | 140.12 |
| esium | 55 | Cs | 132.9054 |
| hlorine | 17 | Cl | 35.453 |
| hromium | 24 | Cr | 51.996 |
| obalt | 27 | Co | 58.9332 |
| opper | 29 | Cu | 63.546 |
| urium | 96 | Cm | 247.703* |
| ysprosium | 66 | Dy | 162.5 |
| insteinium | 99 | Es | 254.0880* |
| rbium | 68 | Er | 167.26 |
| uropium | 63 | Eu | 151.96 |
| ermium | 100 | Fm | 257.0951* |

| Name | Atomic No. | Symbol | Atomic weight |
|------|-----------|--------|---------------|
| Fluorine | 9 | F | 18.9984 |
| Francium | 87 | Fr | 223.0197* |
| Gadolinium | 64 | Gd | 157.25 |
| Gallium | 31 | Ga | 69.72 |
| Germanium | 32 | Ge | 72.59 |
| Gold | 79 | Au | 196.9665 |
| Hafnium | 72 | Hf | 178.49 |
| Helium | 2 | He | 4.0026 |
| Holmium | 67 | Ho | 164.9304 |
| Hydrogen | 1 | H | 1.0079 |
| Indium | 49 | In | 114.82 |
| Iodine | 53 | I | 126.9045 |
| Iridium | 77 | Ir | 192.22 |
| Iron | 26 | Fe | 55.847 |
| Krypton | 36 | Kr | 83.8 |
| Lanthanum | 57 | La | 138.9055 |
| Lawrencium | 103 | Lr | 260.105* |
| Lead | 82 | Pb | 207.19 |
| Lithium | 3 | Li | 6.941 |
| Lutetium | 71 | Lu | 174.97 |
| Magnesium | 12 | Mg | 24.305 |
| Manganese | 25 | Mn | 54.938 |
| Mendelevium | 101 | Md | 258.099* |
| Mercury | 80 | Hg | 200.59 |

| Name | Atomic No. | Symbol | Atomic weight |
|---|---|---|---|
| Molybdenum | 42 | Mo | 95.94 |
| Neodymium | 60 | Nd | 144.24 |
| Neon | 10 | Ne | 20.179 |
| Neptunium | 93 | Np | 237.0482* |
| Nickel | 28 | Ni | 58.71 |
| Niobium | 41 | Nb | 92.9064 |
| Nitrogen | 7 | N | 14.0067 |
| Nobelium | 102 | No | 259.101* |
| Osmium | 76 | Os | 190.2 |
| Oxygen | 8 | O | 15.9994 |
| Palladium | 46 | Pd | 106.4 |
| Phosphorus | 15 | P | 30.97376 |
| Platinum | 78 | Pt | 195.09 |
| Plutonium | 94 | Pu | 244.0642* |
| Polonium | 84 | Po | 208.9824* |
| Potassium | 19 | K | 39.0983 |
| Praseodymium | 59 | Pr | 140.9077 |
| Promethium | 61 | Pm | 144.9128* |
| Protoactinium | 91 | Pa | 231.0359 |
| Radium | 88 | Ra | 226.0254* |
| Radon | 86 | Rn | 222.0176* |
| Rhenium | 75 | Re | 186.207 |
| Rhodium | 45 | Rh | 102.9055 |
| Rubidium | 37 | Rb | 85.4678 |

| Name | Atomic No. | Symbol | Atomic weight |
|------|-----------|--------|---------------|
| Ruthenium | 44 | Ru | 101.07 |
| Samarium | 62 | Sm | 150.35 |
| Scandium | 21 | Sc | 44.9559 |
| Selenium | 34 | Se | 78.96 |
| Silicon | 14 | Si | 28.0855 |
| Silver | 47 | Ag | 107.868 |
| Sodium | 11 | Na | 22.98977 |
| Strontium | 38 | Sr | 87.62 |
| Sulfur | 16 | S | 32.064 |
| Tantalum | 73 | Ta | 180.9479 |
| Technetium | 43 | Tc | 96.9064* |
| Tellurium | 52 | Te | 127.6 |
| Terbium | 65 | Tb | 158.9254 |
| Thallium | 81 | Tl | 204.37 |
| Thorium | 90 | Th | 232.0381 |
| Thulium | 69 | Tm | 168.9342 |
| Tin | 50 | Sn | 118.69 |
| Titanium | 22 | Ti | 47.9 |
| Tungsten | 74 | W | 183.85 |
| Unnilennium | 109 | Une | 266* |
| Unnilhexium | 106 | Unh | 263.120* |
| Unniloctium | 108 | Uno | 265 |
| Unnilpentium | 105 | Unp | 262.114* |
| Unnilquadium | 104 | Ung | 261.109* |
| Unnilseptium | 107 | Uns | 262* |

| | | | |
|---|---|---|---|
| Uranium | 92 | U | 238.029* |
| Vanadium | 23 | V | 50.9414 |
| Xenon | 54 | Xe | 131.3 |
| Ytterbium | 70 | Yb | 173.04 |
| Yttrium | 39 | Y | 88.9059 |
| Zinc | 30 | Zn | 65.381 |
| Zirconium | 40 | Zr | 91.22 |

## BY LETTER SYMBOL

| Atomic Symbol | No. | Name | Atomic weight |
|---|---|---|---|
| Ac | 89 | Actinium | 227.0278* |
| Ag | 47 | Silver | 107.868 |
| Al | 13 | Aluminum | 26.98154 |
| Am | 95 | Americium | 243.0614* |
| Ar | 18 | Argon | 39.948 |
| As | 33 | Arsenic | 74.9216 |
| At | 85 | Astatine | 209.9870* |
| Au | 79 | Gold | 196.9665 |
| B | 5 | Boron | 10.81 |
| Ba | 56 | Barium | 137.33 |
| Be | 4 | Beryllium | 9.01218 |
| Bk | 97 | Berkelium | 247.0703* |
| Bi | 83 | Bismuth | 208.9804 |
| Br | 35 | Bromine | 79.904 |

| Atomic Symbol | No. | Name | Atomic weight |
|---|---|---|---|
| C | 6 | Carbon | 12.011 |
| Ca | 20 | Calcium | 40.08 |
| Cd | 48 | Cadmium | 112.41 |
| Ce | 58 | Cerium | 140.12 |
| Cf | 98 | Californium | 251.0796* |
| Cl | 17 | Chlorine | 35.453 |
| Cm | 96 | Curium | 247.0703* |
| Co | 27 | Cobalt | 58.9332 |
| Cr | 24 | Chromium | 51.996 |
| Cs | 55 | Cesium | 132.9054 |
| Cu | 29 | Copper | 63.546 |
| Dy | 66 | Dysprosium | 162.5 |
| Er | 68 | Erbium | 167.26 |
| Es | 99 | Einsteinium | 254.088* |
| Eu | 63 | Europium | 151.96 |
| F | 9 | Fluorine | 18.9984 |
| Fe | 26 | Iron | 55.847 |
| Fm | 100 | Fermium | 257.0951* |
| Fr | 87 | Francium | 223.0197* |
| Ga | 31 | Gallium | 69.72 |
| Gd | 64 | Gadolinium | 157.25 |
| Ge | 32 | Germanium | 72.59 |
| H | 1 | Hydrogen | 1.0079 |
| He | 2 | Helium | 4.0026 |
| Hf | 72 | Hafnium | 178.49 |

| Atomic Symbol | No. | Name | Atomic weight |
|---|---|---|---|
| Hg | 80 | Mercury | 200.59 |
| Ho | 67 | Holmium | 164.9304 |
| | 53 | Iodine | 126.9045 |
| In | 49 | Indium | 114.82 |
| Ir | 77 | Iridium | 192.22 |
| K | 19 | Potassium | 39.0983 |
| Kr | 36 | Krypton | 83.8 |
| La | 57 | Lanthanum | 138.9055 |
| Li | 3 | Lithium | 6.941 |
| Lr | 103 | Lawrencium | 260.105* |
| Lu | 71 | Lutetium | 174.97 |
| Md | 101 | Mendelevium | 258.099* |
| Mg | 12 | Magnesium | 24.305 |
| Mn | 25 | Manganese | 54.938 |
| Mo | 42 | Molybdenum | 95.94 |
| N | 7 | Nitrogen | 14.0007 |
| Na | 11 | Sodium | 22.98977 |
| Nb | 41 | Niobium | 92.9064 |
| Nd | 60 | Neodymium | 144.24 |
| Ne | 10 | Neon | 20.179 |
| Ni | 28 | Nickel | 58.71 |
| No | 102 | Nobelium | 259.101* |
| Np | 93 | Neptunium | 237.0482* |
| O | 8 | Oxygen | 15.9994 |
| Os | 76 | Osmium | 190.2 |

| Atomic Symbol | No. | Name | Atomic weight |
|---|---|---|---|
| P | 15 | Phosphorus | 30.97376 |
| Pa | 91 | Protoactinium | 231.0359 |
| Pb | 82 | Lead | 207.19 |
| Pd | 46 | Palladium | 106.4 |
| Pm | 61 | Promethium | 144.9128* |
| Po | 84 | Polonium | 208.9824* |
| Pr | 59 | Praseodymium | 140.9077 |
| Pt | 78 | Platinum | 195.09 |
| Pu | 94 | Plutonium | 244.0642* |
| Ra | 88 | Radium | 226.0254* |
| Rb | 37 | Rubidium | 85.4678 |
| Re | 75 | Rhenium | 186.207 |
| Rh | 45 | Rhodium | 102.9055 |
| Rn | 86 | Radon | 222.0176* |
| Ru | 44 | Ruthenium | 101.07 |
| S | 16 | Sulfur | 32.064 |
| Sb | 51 | Antimony | 121.75 |
| Sc | 21 | Scandium | 44.9559 |
| Se | 34 | Selenium | 78.96 |
| Si | 14 | Silicon | 28.0855 |
| Sm | 62 | Samarium | 150.35 |
| Sn | 50 | Tin | 118.69 |
| Sr | 38 | Strontium | 87.62 |
| Ta | 73 | Tantalum | 180.9479 |
| Tb | 65 | Terbium | 158.9254 |

| Atomic Symbol | No. | Name | Atomic weight |
| --- | --- | --- | --- |
| Tc | 43 | Technetium | 96.9064* |
| Te | 52 | Tellurium | 127.6 |
| Th | 90 | Thorium | 232.0381 |
| Ti | 22 | Titanium | 47.9 |
| Ti | 81 | Thallium | 204.37 |
| Tm | 69 | Thulium | 168.9342 |
| U | 92 | Uranium | 238.029* |
| Une | 109 | Unnilennium | 266* |
| Unh | 106 | Unnilhexium | 263.120* |
| Uno | 108 | Unniloctium | 265 |
| Unp | 105 | Unnilpentium | 262.114* |
| Ung | 104 | Unnilquadium | 261.109* |
| Uns | 107 | Unnilseptium | 262* |
| V | 23 | Vanadium | 50.9414 |
| W | 74 | Tungsten | 183.85 |
| Xe | 54 | Xenon | 131.3 |
| Y | 39 | Yttrium | 88.9059 |
| Yb | 70 | Ytterbium | 173.04 |
| Zn | 30 | Zinc | 65.381 |
| Zr | 40 | Zirconium | 91.22 |

### Scales of hardness

Solids vary in their degree of hardness, which indicates their resistance to being scratched or cut.
The first is Mohs' scale, which is used to measure the relative hardness of ten common minerals. Each of these minerals is assigned a numerical value from 1 to 10: the higher the number, the harder the mineral. Order is determined by the ability of a mineral to scratch all those that have a lower number and to be scratched by those with a higher number. Once this is established, it is possible to place all other minerals on the scale by means of the same scratching procedure.

The second method to determine hardness is the Knoop scale. The Knoop scale gives absolute rather than relative measurements. Readings on this scale are made by measuring the size of the indentation made by a diamond-shaped device dropped on the material being tested. Again, the higher the number the harder the substance, but the intervals between minerals and levels of hardness differ greatly from scale to scale. Minerals with values between 1 and 7 on Mohs' scale fall below 1,000 on the Knoop scale, and between 8 and 9 fall below 2,000. Diamond fall at 7,000.

The third scale is called the Common-object scale. A simple way of measuring hardness uses common objects, whose hardness on the Mohs' scale is known:

fingernail (2-2.5 Mohs')
coin (4)
) knife blade (5-6)
) knife sharpener (8-9)

# CHAPTER 4

# TIME

As the saying goes, time is on our side. Or is it? Ever since the Industrial Age, it seems that we have been working for the clock, instead of working against it. In this chapter you might even find a way to find more free time (hint: switch to a thirteen month calendar!).

## Astronomical time

Throughout the course of history, different cultures have developed unique ways to measure time. The earliest civilizations measured time by motion; specifically, the motion of the Earth, Sun, Moon, and stars. Today, these early measurements have been identified and quantified using our more modern, and familiar terms.

*Anomalistic time* refers to the time interval between two consecutive pawssages of the Earth around the Sun measured at its closest point.

*Sidereal time* refers to a modern calculation where the Earth's position is notated according to a fixed star, taking into account the Earth's orbit in relation to the Sun.

*Tropical time* refers to the apparent passage of the Sun and the actual passage of the Moon across the Earth's equatorial plane. A tropical year is measured from one vernal equinox to the next.

A *synodic month* is based on the phases of the Moon. A mean solar day refers to individual periods of darkness and light averaged over a year.

| Name | Days | Hrs | Minutes | Seconds |
|---|---|---|---|---|
| sidereal year | 365 | 6 | 9 | 10 |
| anomalistic year | 365 | 6 | 13 | 53 |
| tropical year | 365 | 5 | 48 | 45 |
| sidereal month | 27 | 7 | 43 | 11 |
| tropical month | 27 | 7 | 43 | 5 |
| synodic month | 29 | 12 | 44 | 3 |
| mean solar day | 0 | 24 | 0 | 0 |
| sidereal day | 0 | 23 | 56 | 4 |

# quinox and solstice

nce used for religious ceremonies, these occurences
ctually have a very accurate, scientific measurement.
he inclination of the Earth to its plane of rotation
round the Sun produces variations in the lengths of
ays and nights at different times of the year.
olstices occur when the Sun appears to be overhead
t midday at the maximum distances north and south
f the Equator. Right before the summer solstice,
ays are longest and nights are shortest. For the win-
r solstice, this is reversed.

Equinoxes are when day and night are equal
verywhere; at these times, the Sun appears overhead
t midday at the Equator.

The following list includes the dates of the sol-
ices and equinox in each hemisphere:

| ate | Northern | Southern |
| --- | --- | --- |
| ine 21 | summer solstice | winter solstice |
| ept. 23 | autumnal equinox | vernal equinox |
| ec. 22 | winter solstice | summer solstice |
| larch 21 | vernal equinox | autumnal equinox |

### *Seasons*

Seasons refer to weather related variations, and are the result of the inclination of the Earth's axis to its plane of rotation around the Sun. As the Earth rotates, parts of the globe are tilted away from the Sun and receive less radiant energy than those receiving rays more directly. If you are at a point closer to the Equator or at the polar regions, the regional climate would hardly be affected by the changing seasons, because there is little difference in the degree of the Earth's position to the Sun.

| **Northern** | **Southern** |
|---|---|
| summer | winter |
| fall | spring |
| winter | summer |
| spring | fall |

### *Length of days*

The following illustrates the variety in the length of one day at different latitudes. On this particular day (the summer solstice: June 21st), the northern hemisphere receives the maximum hours of daylight; the southern hemisphere, the minimum.

| Location | Degrees Latitude | Daylight Hrs |
|---|---|---|
| Arctic Circle | 660 33'N | 24 hours |
| The Equator: | 00 | 12 hours |
| Antarctic Circle | 660 33'S | 0 hours daylight |

## Artificial time

As cultures evolved, so did the need for creating a system in which time fit into a repeatable and sustainable schedule. The astronomic system comprised of years and seasons was broken down into smaller units of weeks and months. Days were further divided into hours, minutes, and seconds, until we have the system we use now. All of this time is considered to be artificial, in that it was a new system imposed to fit based on the astronomical model.

| Artificial Name | Duration |
|---|---|
| Week | 7 days |
| Month | 28-31 days |
| Season | 3 months |
| Year | 12 months; 52 weeks; 365 days |
| Leap Year | 366 days |
| Decade | 10 years |
| Century | 100 years |
| Millennium | 1,000 years |

### Days, hours, minutes

Below are listed the basic subdivisions of a day:

1 day = 24 hours = 1,440 minutes = 86,400 seconds
1 hour = 1/24 day = 60 minutes = 3,600 seconds
1 minute = 1/1,440 day = 1/60 hour = 60 seconds
1 second = 1/86,400 day= 1/3,600 hour = 1/60 minute

### Seconds

Today, even greater precision in measuring time has required seconds to be broken down even further into smaller units, using standard metric prefixes:

| Name | Duration |
| --- | --- |
| 1 terasecond (Ts) | 31,689 years |
| 1 gigasecond (Gs) | 31.7 years |
| 1 megasecond (Ms) | 11.6 days |
| 1 kilosecond (ks) | 16.67 minutes |
| 1 millisecond (ms) | 0.001 seconds |
| 1 microsecond (gs) | 0.000001 seconds |
| 1 nanosecond (ns) | 0.000000001 seconds |
| 1 picosecond (ps) | 0.000000000001 seconds |
| 1 femtosecond (fs) | 0.000000000000001 seconds |
| 1 attosecond (as) 10 | 0.000000000000000001 seconds |

## Greenwich Mean Time

To further complicate matters, science and industry have imposed a world clock, so that hours can be compared throughout the world. There are 25 integer World Time Zones from -12 through 0 (GMT) to +12. Each one is 15∞ of longitude as measured East and West from the Prime Meridian in Greenwich, England. For each longitudinal measurement, one hour is added or subtracted from Greenwich Mean time.

There are both civilian designations which are typically three letter abbreviations (e.g. EST) for most time zones. In addition there are military designations. These use each letter of the alphabet (except 'J') and are known by their phonetic equivalent. E.G. Greenwich Mean Time (civilian) or Z = Zulu (military and aviation).

## U.S. Standard Times: EST, CST, MST, PST

In a country as large as the U.S., further time zones had to be incorporated. With the Standard Time Act of 1918, Congress defined four additional times zones within the U.S. Today, there are nine U.S. time zones that include Eastern, Central, Mountain, Pacific, Alaska, Hawaii-Aleutian, Samoa, Wake Island, and Guam.

The four primary time zones for the contigous U.S.–Eastern, Central, Mountain, Pacific–each run one hour behind its closest zone. The following table illustrates this point:

| Zone | Time |
|------|------|
| EST | 1:00 P.M. |
| CST | 12:00 P.M. (noon) |
| MST | 11:00 A.M. |
| PST | 10:00 A.M. |

## International Office Time

The following is a list of standard office hours in various cities around the world. You'll note that many countries "close down" for several hours during each work day for a long lunch respit.

| City | Business Day |
|------|--------------|
| Athens | 8:00 A.M. - 2:00 P.M., 2:00 P.M. - 6:00 P.M. |
| Brussels | 8:30 A.M. - 12:00 P.M., 2:30 P.M. - 5:30 P.M. |
| Copenhagen | 8:00 A.M. - 4:30 P.M. |
| Dublin | 9:30 A.M. - 5:30 P.M. |
| Frankfurt | 8:00 A.M. - 5:30 P.M. |
| Geneva | 8:00 A.M. - 12:00 P.M., 2:00 P.M. - 6:00 P.M. |
| Johannesburg | 8:30 A.M. - 5:00 P.M. |
| Lisbon | 10:00 A.M. - 12:30 P.M., 2:30 P.M. - 6:00 P.M. |
| London | 9:00 A.M. - 5:00 P.M. |
| Madrid | 9:30 A.M. - 1:30 P.M., 3:00 P.M. - 6:00 P.M. |

| Milan | 8:30 A.M. - 12:45 P.M., 3:00 P.M. - 6:30 P.M. |
| New York | 9:00 A.M. - 5:00 P.M. |
| Paris | 9:00 A.M. - 4:30 P.M. |
| Riyadh | 8:00 A.M. - 1:00 P.M., 5:00 P.M. - 8:00 P.M. |
| Stockholm | 8:30 A.M. - 5:00 P.M. |
| Sydney | 9:00 A.M. - 5:00 P.M. |
| Tokyo | 9:00 A.M. - 5:00 P.M. |
| Toronto | 8:30 A.M. - 5:30 P.M. |

## Daylight Saving Time

The phrase "Spring forward, fall back" can help you remember how Daylight Saving Time affects your clock. At 2 A.M. on the first Sunday in April, we set our clocks forward one hour ahead of standard time ("spring forward"). We "fall back" at 2 A.M. on the last Sunday in October by setting our clock back one hour, then returning to standard time. The change to Daylight Saving Time allows us to use less energy in lighting our homes by taking advantage of the longer and later daylight hours.

Daylight Saving Time was instituted in the U.S. during World War I in order to save energy for war production by taking advantage of the later hours of daylight between April and October. During World War II the federal government again required the states to observe the time change. Between the wars and after World War II, states chose whether or not to observe Daylight Saving Time. In 1966, Congress passed the Uniform Time Act which standardized the length of Daylight Saving Time. However, Arizona, Hawaii, parts of Indiana, Puerto Rico, the U.S. Virgin Islands, and American Samoa have chosen not to observe Daylight Saving Time.

Other parts of the world have adopted their own Daylight Saving Time as well. For example, the European Union (EU) standardized a EU-wide "summertime period." The EU version of Daylight Saving Time runs from the last Sunday in March through the last Sunday in October.

During the six-and-a-half-month period of U.S. Daylight Saving Time, the names of each time zone changes as well. Eastern Standard Time (EST) becomes Eastern Daylight Time, Central Standard Time (CST) becomes Central Daylight Time (CDT), Mountain Standard Time (MST) becomes Mountain Daylight Tome (MDT), Pacific Standard Time becomes Pacific Daylight Time (PDT).

## Calendars

Various cultures have developed their own calendars. At present, there are three main calendars in use:

### GREGORIAN

The Gregorian calendar is a 16th-century adaptation of the Julian calendar, which was devised in the 1st century BC. This calendar is based on the solar year, which lasts 365 1/4 days. In this system, years whose number is not divisible by 4 have 365 days, as do centennial years unless the figures before the zeros are divisible by 4. All other years have 366 days; these are leap years.

Below are the names of the months and number of days for a non-leap year:

| Month | Number of Days |
|---|---|
| January | 31 |
| February | 28 |
| March | 31 |
| April | 30 |
| May | 31 |
| June | 30 |
| July | 31 |
| August | 31 |
| September | 30 |
| October | 31 |
| November | 30 |
| December | 31 |

## JEWISH

A year in the Jewish calendar has 13 months if its number, when divided by 9, leaves 0, 3, 6, 8, 11, 14, or 17; otherwise, it has 12 months. The Jewish calendar is based on the cycle of the moon around the Earth. The length of this cycle, the lunar month, is about 29 1/2 days. Twelve lunar months make therefore about 354 days, which is 11 1/4 days shorter than the solar year.

In biblical times, the arrival of the new month was determined by watching the phase of the moon. However in modern times a fixed calendar is used in which the length of the months alternates between 29 and 30 days.

The difference of 11 1/4 days between 12 lunar months and one solar year accumulates in three years to more than a month. If no adjustments are made, a summer month could shift to the winter. Because the Jewish holidays are closely related to the seasons (for example, Jews are commanded to celebrate Passover in the spring), an adjustment to the calendar must be made every few years. Every two or three years one extra month is added to a year. Such a year is called a leap year and it has two months of Adar. In 13-month years, the month Adar 2, with 29 days, falls between Adar and Nisan. There is a nineteen year cycle which determines when a year is a leap year.

Below are the months and number of days in each for the Hebrew year 5762:

| Month | Number of Days |
|-------|----------------|
| Tishrei | 30 days |
| Cheshvan | 29/30 days |
| Kislev | 29/30 days |
| Tevet | 29 days |
| Shvat | 30 days |
| Adar 1 | 30 days |
| Adar 2 | 29 days |
| Nisan | 30 days |
| Iyyar | 29 days |
| Sivan | 30 days |
| Tamuz | 29 days |
| Av | 30 days |
| Elul | 29 days |

## MUSLIM

A year in the Muslim calendar (or Hijri calendar) has 355 days if its number, when divided by 30, leaves 2, 5, 7, 10, 13, 16, 18, 21, 24, 26, or 29; otherwise it has 354 days. Unlike the Jewish calendar it is based on a purely lunar cycle. Each month starts when the lunar crescent is first seen (by a human observer's eye) after a new moon.

The Muslim calendar has 12 months comprised of either 30 and 29 days. This results in the calendar rotating around the seasons in a 30-year cycle. The era is counted as beginning on the day Muhammad migrated from Mecca in 622 A.D.

The calendar is based on the Qur'an and its proper observance is a sacred duty for Muslims. It is the official calendar in countries around the Gulf, especially Saudi Arabia. But other Muslim countries use the Gregorian calendar for civil purposes and only turn to the Islamic calendar for religious purposes.

Below are the names of the months for the Muslim year:

**Month**
Muharram
Rajab
Safar
Shaban
Rabi-Ul-Awwal
Ramazan
Rabi-Us-Saani
Shawwal
Jamadi-Ul-Awwal
Ziqa'ad
Jamadi-Us-Saani
Zilhaj

# Astrology and the zodiac year

The Zodiac has been a part of various cultures for thousands of years. The practice of astrology links the month, time, and location in which you were born to the position of the stars. From this information, and variety of personality traits can be culled. The most notable are:

**Sign: Aries**
Symbol: Ram
Dates: (March 21- April 20)
Trait: a pioneer spirit

**Sign: Taurus**
Symbol: Bull
Dates: (April 21- May 20)
Trait: a model of perseverance

**Sign: Gemini**
Symbol: Twins
Dates: (May 21-June 20)
Trait: embraces versatility

**Sign: Cancer**
Symbol: Crab
Dates: (June 21-July 21)
Trait: Strong nurturers

**Sign: Leo**
Symbol: Lion
Dates: (July 22-August 21)
Trait: Powerful leaders

**Sign: Virgo**
Symbol: Virgin
Dates: (August 22-September 21)
Trait: Detail-oriented

**Sign: Libra**
Symbol: Scales
Dates: (September 22- October 22)
Trait: Present a balanced perspective

**Sign: Scorpio**
Symbol: Scorpion
Dates: (October 23- November 21)
Trait: Curious and dilligent

**Sign: Sagittarius**
Symbol: Archer
Dates: (November 22-December 20)
Trait: Idealists

**Sign: Capricorn**
Symbol: Goat
Dates: (December 21-January 19)
Trait: Master self-discipline

**Sign: Aquarius**
Symbol: Water-bearer
Dates: (January 20-February 18)
Trait: Original thinkers

**Sign: Pisces**
Symbol: Fish
Dates: (February 19-March 20)
Trait: Emotionally-driven

## Anniversaries

| Year | Traditional | Modern |
|------|-------------|--------|
| 1st | Paper | Clocks |
| 2nd | Cotton | China |
| 3rd | Leather | Crystal or glass |
| 4th | Linen | Electrical appliances |
| 5th | Wood | Silverware |
| 6th | Iron | Wood |
| 7th | Wool | Desk sets |
| 8th | Bronze | Linen, lace |
| 9th | Pottery | Leather |
| 10th | Aluminum | Diamond jewelry |
| 11th | Steel | Fashion accessories |
| 12th | Silk | Pearls or colored gems |
| 13th | Lace | Furs |
| 14th | Ivory | Gold Jewelry |
| 15th | Crystal | Watches |
| 20th | China | Platinum |
| 25th | Silver | Sterling silver |
| 30th | Pearl | Diamond |
| 35th | Coral | Jade |
| 40th | Ruby | Ruby |
| 45th | Sapphire | Sapphire |
| 50th | Gold | Gold |
| 55th | Emerald | Emerald |
| 60th | Diamond | Diamond |

# The Perpetual calendar

A perpetual calendar is a tool to help you discover on which day of the week a particular date fell on. The one below is good for any date between the years 1780 and 2046. Simply look up the year in the key and the letter shown to the right will indicate which of the calendars to consult.

## Key:

| | | | | | | | |
|------|---|------|---|------|---|------|---|
| 1780 | N | 1797 | A | 1814 | G | 1831 | G |
| 1781 | B | 1798 | B | 1815 | A | 1832 | H |
| 1782 | C | 1799 | C | 1816 | I | 1833 | C |
| 1783 | D | 1800 | D | 1817 | D | 1834 | D |
| 1784 | L | 1801 | E | 1818 | E | 1835 | E |
| 1785 | G | 1802 | F | 1819 | F | 1836 | M |
| 1786 | A | 1803 | G | 1820 | N | 1837 | A |
| 1787 | B | 1804 | H | 1821 | B | 1838 | B |
| 1788 | J | 1805 | C | 1822 | C | 1839 | C |
| 1789 | E | 1806 | D | 1823 | D | 1840 | K |
| 1790 | F | 1807 | E | 1824 | L | 1841 | F |
| 1791 | G | 1808 | M | 1825 | G | 1842 | G |
| 1792 | H | 1809 | A | 1826 | A | 1843 | A |
| 1793 | C | 1810 | B | 1827 | B | 1844 | I |
| 1794 | D | 1811 | C | 1828 | J | 1845 | D |
| 1795 | E | 812 | K | 1829 | E | 1846 | E |
| 1796 | M | 1813 | F | 1830 | F | 1847 | F |

| | | | | | | |
|---|---|---|---|---|---|---|---|
| 1848 | N | 1874 | E | 1900 | B | 1926 | |
| 1849 | B | 1875 | F | 1901 | C | 1927 | |
| 1850 | C | 1876 | N | 1902 | D | 1928 | |
| 1851 | D | 1877 | B | 1903 | E | 1929 | |
| 1852 | L | 1878 | C | 1904 | M | 1930 | |
| 1853 | G | 1879 | D | 1905 | A | 1931 | |
| 1854 | A | 1880 | L | 1906 | B | 1932 | |
| 1855 | B | 1881 | G | 1907 | C | 1933 | |
| 1856 | J | 1882 | A | 1908 | K | 1934 | |
| 1857 | E | 1883 | B | 1909 | F | 1935 | |
| 1858 | F | 1884 | J | 1910 | G | 1936 | |
| 1859 | G | 1885 | E | 1911 | A | 1937 | |
| 1860 | H | 1886 | F | 1912 | I | 1938 | |
| 1861 | C | 1887 | G | 1913 | D | 1939 | |
| 1862 | D | 1888 | H | 1914 | E | 1940 | |
| 1863 | E | 1889 | C | 1915 | F | 1941 | |
| 1864 | M | 1890 | D | 1916 | N | 1942 | |
| 1865 | A | 1891 | E | 1917 | B | 1943 | |
| 1866 | B | 1892 | M | 1918 | C | 1944 | |
| 1867 | C | 1893 | A | 1919 | D | 1945 | |
| 1868 | K | 1894 | B | 1920 | L | 1946 | |
| 1869 | F | 1895 | C | 1921 | G | 1947 | |
| 1870 | G | 1896 | K | 1922 | A | 1948 | |
| 1871 | A | 1897 | F | 1923 | B | 1949 | |
| 1872 | I | 1898 | G | 1924 | J | 1950 | |
| 1873 | D | 899 | A | 1925 | E | 1951 | |

| | | | | | | | |
|---|---|---|---|---|---|---|---|
| 952 | J | 1978 | A | 2004 | L | 2030 | C |
| 953 | E | 1979 | B | 2005 | G | 2031 | D |
| 954 | F | 1980 | J | 2006 | A | 2032 | L |
| 955 | G | 1981 | E | 2007 | B | 2033 | G |
| 956 | H | 1982 | F | 2008 | J | 2034 | A |
| 957 | C | 1983 | G | 2009 | E | 2035 | B |
| 958 | D | 1984 | H | 2010 | F | 2036 | J |
| 959 | E | 1985 | C | 2011 | G | 2037 | E |
| 960 | M | 1986 | D | 2012 | H | 2038 | F |
| 961 | A | 1987 | E | 2013 | C | 2039 | G |
| 962 | B | 1988 | M | 2014 | D | 2040 | H |
| 963 | C | 1989 | A | 2015 | E | 2041 | C |
| 964 | K | 1990 | B | 2016 | M | 2042 | D |
| 965 | F | 1991 | C | 2017 | A | 2043 | E |
| 966 | G | 1992 | K | 2018 | B | 2044 | M |
| 967 | A | 1993 | F | 2019 | C | 2045 | A |
| 968 | I | 1994 | G | 2020 | K | 2046 | B |
| 969 | D | 1995 | A | 2021 | F | | |
| 970 | E | 1996 | I | 2022 | G | | |
| 971 | F | 1997 | D | 2023 | A | | |
| 972 | N | 1998 | E | 2024 | I | | |
| 973 | B | 1999 | F | 2025 | D | | |
| 974 | C | 2000 | N | 2026 | E | | |
| 975 | D | 2001 | B | 2027 | F | | |
| 976 | L | 2002 | C | 2028 | N | | |
| 977 | G | 2003 | D | 2029 | B | | |

**A** 1786 1797 1809 1815 1826 1837 1843
1854 1865 1871 1882 1893 1899 1905

## JANUARY

| S | M | T | W | T | F | S |
|---|---|---|---|---|---|---|
| 1 | 2 | 3 | 4 | 5 | 6 | 7 |
| 8 | 9 | 10 | 11 | 12 | 13 | 14 |
| 15 | 16 | 17 | 18 | 19 | 20 | 21 |
| 22 | 23 | 24 | 25 | 26 | 27 | 28 |
| 29 | 30 | 31 | | | | |

## FEBRUARY

| S | M | T | W | T | F | S |
|---|---|---|---|---|---|---|
| | | | 1 | 2 | 3 | 4 |
| 5 | 6 | 7 | 8 | 9 | 10 | 11 |
| 12 | 13 | 14 | 15 | 16 | 17 | 18 |
| 19 | 20 | 21 | 22 | 23 | 24 | 25 |
| 26 | 27 | 28 | | | | |

## MARCH

| S | M | T | W | T | F | S |
|---|---|---|---|---|---|---|
| | | | 1 | 2 | 3 | 4 |
| 5 | 6 | 7 | 8 | 9 | 10 | 11 |
| 12 | 13 | 14 | 15 | 16 | 17 | 18 |
| 19 | 20 | 21 | 22 | 23 | 24 | 25 |
| 26 | 27 | 28 | 29 | 30 | 31 | |

## APRIL

| S | M | T | W | T | F | S |
|---|---|---|---|---|---|---|
| | | | | | | 1 |
| 2 | 3 | 4 | 5 | 6 | 7 | 8 |
| 9 | 10 | 11 | 12 | 13 | 14 | 15 |
| 16 | 17 | 18 | 19 | 20 | 21 | 22 |
| 23 | 24 | 25 | 26 | 27 | 28 | 29 |
| 30 | | | | | | |

## MAY

| S | M | T | W | T | F | S |
|---|---|---|---|---|---|---|
| | 1 | 2 | 3 | 4 | 5 | 6 |
| 7 | 8 | 9 | 10 | 11 | 12 | 13 |
| 14 | 15 | 16 | 17 | 18 | 19 | 20 |
| 21 | 22 | 23 | 24 | 25 | 26 | 27 |
| 28 | 29 | 30 | 31 | | | |

## JUNE

| S | M | T | W | T | F | S |
|---|---|---|---|---|---|---|
| | | | | 1 | 2 | 3 |
| 4 | 5 | 6 | 7 | 8 | 9 | 10 |
| 11 | 12 | 13 | 14 | 15 | 16 | 17 |
| 18 | 19 | 20 | 21 | 22 | 23 | 24 |
| 25 | 26 | 27 | 28 | 29 | 30 | |

**1911 1922 1933 1939 1950 1961 1967
1978 1989 1995 2006 2017 2023 2034
2045** **A**

## JULY

| S | M | T | W | T | F | S |
|---|---|---|---|---|---|---|
| | | | | | | 1 |
| 2 | 3 | 4 | 5 | 6 | 7 | 8 |
| 9 | 10 | 11 | 12 | 13 | 14 | 15 |
| 16 | 17 | 18 | 19 | 20 | 21 | 22 |
| 23 | 24 | 25 | 26 | 27 | 28 | 29 |
| 30 | 31 | | | | | |

## AUGUST

| S | M | T | W | T | F | S |
|---|---|---|---|---|---|---|
| | | 1 | 2 | 3 | 4 | 5 |
| 6 | 7 | 8 | 9 | 10 | 11 | 12 |
| 13 | 14 | 15 | 16 | 17 | 18 | 19 |
| 20 | 21 | 22 | 23 | 24 | 25 | 26 |
| 27 | 28 | 29 | 30 | 31 | | |

## SEPTEMBER

| S | M | T | W | T | F | S |
|---|---|---|---|---|---|---|
| | | | | | 1 | 2 |
| 3 | 4 | 5 | 6 | 7 | 8 | 9 |
| 10 | 11 | 12 | 13 | 14 | 15 | 16 |
| 17 | 18 | 19 | 20 | 21 | 22 | 23 |
| 24 | 25 | 26 | 27 | 28 | 29 | 30 |

## OCTOBER

| S | M | T | W | T | F | S |
|---|---|---|---|---|---|---|
| 1 | 2 | 3 | 4 | 5 | 6 | 7 |
| 8 | 9 | 10 | 11 | 12 | 13 | 14 |
| 15 | 16 | 17 | 18 | 19 | 20 | 21 |
| 22 | 23 | 24 | 25 | 26 | 27 | 28 |
| 29 | 30 | 31 | | | | |

## NOVEMBER

| S | M | T | W | T | F | S |
|---|---|---|---|---|---|---|
| | | | 1 | 2 | 3 | 4 |
| 5 | 6 | 7 | 8 | 9 | 10 | 11 |
| 12 | 13 | 14 | 15 | 16 | 17 | 18 |
| 19 | 20 | 21 | 22 | 23 | 24 | 25 |
| 26 | 27 | 28 | 29 | 30 | | |

## DECEMBER

| S | M | T | W | T | F | S |
|---|---|---|---|---|---|---|
| | | | | | 1 | 2 |
| 3 | 4 | 5 | 6 | 7 | 8 | 9 |
| 10 | 11 | 12 | 13 | 14 | 15 | 16 |
| 17 | 18 | 19 | 20 | 21 | 22 | 23 |
| 24 | 25 | 26 | 27 | 28 | 29 | 30 |
| 31 | | | | | | |

# B

1781 1787 1798 1810 1821 1827 1838
1849 1855 1866 1877 1883 1894 1900

**JANUARY**

| S | M | T | W | T | F | S |
|---|---|---|---|---|---|---|
| | 1 | 2 | 3 | 4 | 5 | 6 |
| 7 | 8 | 9 | 10 | 11 | 12 | 13 |
| 14 | 15 | 16 | 17 | 18 | 19 | 20 |
| 21 | 22 | 23 | 24 | 25 | 26 | 27 |
| 28 | 29 | 30 | 31 | | | |

**FEBRUARY**

| S | M | T | W | T | F | S |
|---|---|---|---|---|---|---|
| | | | | 1 | 2 | 3 |
| 4 | 5 | 6 | 7 | 8 | 9 | 10 |
| 11 | 12 | 13 | 14 | 15 | 16 | 17 |
| 18 | 19 | 20 | 21 | 22 | 23 | 24 |
| 25 | 26 | 27 | 28 | | | |

**MARCH**

| S | M | T | W | T | F | S |
|---|---|---|---|---|---|---|
| | | | | 1 | 2 | 3 |
| 4 | 5 | 6 | 7 | 8 | 9 | 10 |
| 11 | 12 | 13 | 14 | 15 | 16 | 17 |
| 18 | 19 | 20 | 21 | 22 | 23 | 24 |
| 25 | 26 | 27 | 28 | 29 | 30 | 31 |

**APRIL**

| S | M | T | W | T | F | S |
|---|---|---|---|---|---|---|
| 1 | 2 | 3 | 4 | 5 | 6 | 7 |
| 8 | 9 | 10 | 11 | 12 | 13 | 14 |
| 15 | 16 | 17 | 18 | 19 | 20 | 21 |
| 22 | 23 | 24 | 25 | 26 | 27 | 28 |
| 29 | 30 | | | | | |

**MAY**

| S | M | T | W | T | F | S |
|---|---|---|---|---|---|---|
| | | 1 | 2 | 3 | 4 | 5 |
| 6 | 7 | 8 | 9 | 10 | 11 | 12 |
| 13 | 14 | 15 | 16 | 17 | 18 | 19 |
| 20 | 21 | 22 | 23 | 24 | 25 | 26 |
| 27 | 28 | 29 | 30 | 31 | | |

**JUNE**

| S | M | T | W | T | F | S |
|---|---|---|---|---|---|---|
| | | | | | 1 | 2 |
| 3 | 4 | 5 | 6 | 7 | 8 | 9 |
| 10 | 11 | 12 | 13 | 14 | 15 | 16 |
| 17 | 18 | 19 | 20 | 21 | 22 | 23 |
| 24 | 25 | 26 | 27 | 28 | 29 | 30 |

**1906 1917 1923 1934 1945 1951 1962
1973 1979 1990 2001 2007 2018 2029
2035 2046**

# B

## JULY
| S | M | T | W | T | F | S |
|---|---|---|---|---|---|---|
| 1 | 2 | 3 | 4 | 5 | 6 | 7 |
| 8 | 9 | 10 | 11 | 12 | 13 | 14 |
| 15 | 16 | 17 | 18 | 19 | 20 | 21 |
| 22 | 23 | 24 | 25 | 26 | 27 | 28 |
| 29 | 30 | 31 | | | | |

## AUGUST
| S | M | T | W | T | F | S |
|---|---|---|---|---|---|---|
| | | | | 1 | 2 | 3 | 4 |
| 5 | 6 | 7 | 8 | 9 | 10 | 11 |
| 12 | 13 | 14 | 15 | 16 | 17 | 18 |
| 19 | 20 | 21 | 22 | 23 | 24 | 25 |
| 26 | 27 | 28 | 29 | 30 | 31 | |

## SEPTEMBER
| S | M | T | W | T | F | S |
|---|---|---|---|---|---|---|
| | | | | | | 1 |
| 2 | 3 | 4 | 5 | 6 | 7 | 8 |
| 9 | 10 | 11 | 12 | 13 | 14 | 15 |
| 16 | 17 | 18 | 19 | 20 | 21 | 22 |
| 23 | 24 | 25 | 26 | 27 | 28 | 29 |
| 30 | | | | | | |

## OCTOBER
| S | M | T | W | T | F | S |
|---|---|---|---|---|---|---|
| | 1 | 2 | 3 | 4 | 5 | 6 |
| 7 | 8 | 9 | 10 | 11 | 12 | 13 |
| 14 | 15 | 16 | 17 | 18 | 19 | 20 |
| 21 | 22 | 23 | 24 | 25 | 26 | 27 |
| 28 | 29 | 30 | 31 | | | |

## NOVEMBER
| S | M | T | W | T | F | S |
|---|---|---|---|---|---|---|
| | | | | 1 | 2 | 3 |
| 4 | 5 | 6 | 7 | 8 | 9 | 10 |
| 11 | 12 | 13 | 14 | 15 | 16 | 17 |
| 18 | 19 | 20 | 21 | 22 | 23 | 24 |
| 25 | 26 | 27 | 28 | 29 | 30 | |

## DECEMBER
| S | M | T | W | T | F | S |
|---|---|---|---|---|---|---|
| | | | | | | 1 |
| 2 | 3 | 4 | 5 | 6 | 7 | 8 |
| 9 | 10 | 11 | 12 | 13 | 14 | 15 |
| 16 | 17 | 18 | 19 | 20 | 21 | 22 |
| 23 | 24 | 25 | 26 | 27 | 28 | 29 |
| 30 | 31 | | | | | |

# C

**1782 1793 1799 1805 1811 1822 1833**
**1839 1850 1861 1867 1878 1889 1895**

**JANUARY**

| S | M | T | W | T | F | S |
|---|---|---|---|---|---|---|
|   |   | 1 | 2 | 3 | 4 | 5 |
| 6 | 7 | 8 | 9 | 10 | 11 | 12 |
| 13 | 14 | 15 | 16 | 17 | 18 | 19 |
| 20 | 21 | 22 | 23 | 24 | 25 | 26 |
| 27 | 28 | 29 | 30 | 31 |   |   |

**FEBRUARY**

| S | M | T | W | T | F | S |
|---|---|---|---|---|---|---|
|   |   |   |   |   | 1 | 2 |
| 3 | 4 | 5 | 6 | 7 | 8 | 9 |
| 10 | 11 | 12 | 13 | 14 | 15 | 16 |
| 17 | 18 | 19 | 20 | 21 | 22 | 23 |
| 24 | 25 | 26 | 27 | 28 |   |   |

**MARCH**

| S | M | T | W | T | F | S |
|---|---|---|---|---|---|---|
|   |   |   |   |   | 1 | 2 |
| 3 | 4 | 5 | 6 | 7 | 8 | 9 |
| 10 | 11 | 12 | 13 | 14 | 15 | 16 |
| 17 | 18 | 19 | 20 | 21 | 22 | 23 |
| 24 | 25 | 26 | 27 | 28 | 29 | 30 |
| 31 |   |   |   |   |   |   |

**APRIL**

| S | M | T | W | T | F | S |
|---|---|---|---|---|---|---|
|   | 1 | 2 | 3 | 4 | 5 | 6 |
| 7 | 8 | 9 | 10 | 11 | 12 | 13 |
| 14 | 15 | 16 | 17 | 18 | 19 | 20 |
| 21 | 22 | 23 | 24 | 25 | 26 | 27 |
| 28 | 29 | 30 |   |   |   |   |

**MAY**

| S | M | T | W | T | F | S |
|---|---|---|---|---|---|---|
|   |   |   | 1 | 2 | 3 | 4 |
| 5 | 6 | 7 | 8 | 9 | 10 | 11 |
| 12 | 13 | 14 | 15 | 16 | 17 | 18 |
| 19 | 20 | 21 | 22 | 23 | 24 | 25 |
| 26 | 27 | 28 | 29 | 30 | 31 |   |

**JUNE**

| S | M | T | W | T | F | S |
|---|---|---|---|---|---|---|
|   |   |   |   |   |   | 1 |
| 2 | 3 | 4 | 5 | 6 | 7 | 8 |
| 9 | 10 | 11 | 12 | 13 | 14 | 15 |
| 16 | 17 | 18 | 19 | 20 | 21 | 22 |
| 23 | 24 | 25 | 26 | 27 | 28 | 29 |
| 30 |   |   |   |   |   |   |

**1901  1907  1918  1929  1935  1946  1957
1963  1974  1985  1991  2002  2013  2019
2030  2041**  C

### JULY
| S | M | T | W | T | F | S |
|---|---|---|---|---|---|---|
|   |   | 1 | 2 | 3 | 4 | 5 | 6 |
| 7 | 8 | 9 | 10 | 11 | 12 | 13 |
| 14 | 15 | 16 | 17 | 18 | 19 | 20 |
| 21 | 22 | 23 | 24 | 25 | 26 | 27 |
| 28 | 29 | 30 | 31 |   |   |   |

### AUGUST
| S | M | T | W | T | F | S |
|---|---|---|---|---|---|---|
|   |   |   |   |   | 1 | 2 | 3 |
| 4 | 5 | 6 | 7 | 8 | 9 | 10 |
| 11 | 12 | 13 | 14 | 15 | 16 | 17 |
| 18 | 19 | 20 | 21 | 22 | 23 | 24 |
| 25 | 26 | 27 | 28 | 29 | 30 | 31 |

### SEPTEMBER
| S | M | T | W | T | F | S |
|---|---|---|---|---|---|---|
| 1 | 2 | 3 | 4 | 5 | 6 | 7 |
| 8 | 9 | 10 | 11 | 12 | 13 | 14 |
| 15 | 16 | 17 | 18 | 19 | 20 | 21 |
| 22 | 23 | 24 | 25 | 26 | 27 | 28 |
| 29 | 30 |   |   |   |   |   |

### OCTOBER
| S | M | T | W | T | F | S |
|---|---|---|---|---|---|---|
|   |   | 1 | 2 | 3 | 4 | 5 |
| 6 | 7 | 8 | 9 | 10 | 11 | 12 |
| 13 | 14 | 15 | 16 | 17 | 18 | 19 |
| 20 | 21 | 22 | 23 | 24 | 25 | 26 |
| 27 | 28 | 29 | 30 | 31 |   |   |

### NOVEMBER
| S | M | T | W | T | F | S |
|---|---|---|---|---|---|---|
|   |   |   |   |   | 1 | 2 |
| 3 | 4 | 5 | 6 | 7 | 8 | 9 |
| 10 | 11 | 12 | 13 | 14 | 15 | 16 |
| 17 | 18 | 19 | 20 | 21 | 22 | 23 |
| 24 | 25 | 26 | 27 | 28 | 29 | 30 |

### DECEMBER
| S | M | T | W | T | F | S |
|---|---|---|---|---|---|---|
| 1 | 2 | 3 | 4 | 5 | 6 | 7 |
| 8 | 9 | 10 | 11 | 12 | 13 | 14 |
| 15 | 16 | 17 | 18 | 19 | 20 | 21 |
| 22 | 23 | 24 | 25 | 26 | 27 | 28 |
| 29 | 30 | 31 |   |   |   |   |

# D   1783 1794 1800 1806 1817 1823 1834
       1845 1851 1862 1873 1879 1890 1902

## JANUARY
| S | M | T | W | T | F | S |
|---|---|---|---|---|---|---|
|   |   |   |   | 1 | 2 | 3 | 4 |
| 5 | 6 | 7 | 8 | 9 | 10 | 11 |
| 12 | 13 | 14 | 15 | 16 | 17 | 18 |
| 19 | 20 | 21 | 22 | 23 | 24 | 25 |
| 26 | 27 | 28 | 29 | 30 | 31 |   |

## FEBRUARY
| S | M | T | W | T | F | S |
|---|---|---|---|---|---|---|
|   |   |   |   |   |   | 1 |
| 2 | 3 | 4 | 5 | 6 | 7 | 8 |
| 9 | 10 | 11 | 12 | 13 | 14 | 15 |
| 16 | 17 | 18 | 19 | 20 | 21 | 22 |
| 23 | 24 | 25 | 26 | 27 | 28 |   |

## MARCH
| S | M | T | W | T | F | S |
|---|---|---|---|---|---|---|
|   |   |   |   |   |   | 1 |
| 2 | 3 | 4 | 5 | 6 | 7 | 8 |
| 9 | 10 | 11 | 12 | 13 | 14 | 15 |
| 16 | 17 | 18 | 19 | 20 | 21 | 22 |
| 23 | 24 | 25 | 26 | 27 | 28 | 29 |
| 30 | 31 |   |   |   |   |   |

## APRIL
| S | M | T | W | T | F | S |
|---|---|---|---|---|---|---|
|   |   | 1 | 2 | 3 | 4 | 5 |
| 6 | 7 | 8 | 9 | 10 | 11 | 12 |
| 13 | 14 | 15 | 16 | 17 | 18 | 19 |
| 20 | 21 | 22 | 23 | 24 | 25 | 26 |
| 27 | 28 | 29 | 30 |   |   |   |

## MAY
| S | M | T | W | T | F | S |
|---|---|---|---|---|---|---|
|   |   |   |   | 1 | 2 | 3 |
| 4 | 5 | 6 | 7 | 8 | 9 | 10 |
| 11 | 12 | 13 | 14 | 15 | 16 | 17 |
| 18 | 19 | 20 | 21 | 22 | 23 | 24 |
| 25 | 26 | 27 | 28 | 29 | 30 | 31 |

## JUNE
| S | M | T | W | T | F | S |
|---|---|---|---|---|---|---|
| 1 | 2 | 3 | 4 | 5 | 6 | 7 |
| 8 | 9 | 10 | 11 | 12 | 13 | 14 |
| 15 | 16 | 17 | 18 | 19 | 20 | 21 |
| 22 | 23 | 24 | 25 | 26 | 27 | 28 |
| 29 | 30 |   |   |   |   |   |

**1913 1919 1930 1941 1947 1958 1969
1975 1986 1997 2003 2014 2025 2031
2042** **D**

### JULY
| S | M | T | W | T | F | S |
|---|---|---|---|---|---|---|
|   |   | 1 | 2 | 3 | 4 | 5 |
| 6 | 7 | 8 | 9 | 10 | 11 | 12 |
| 13 | 14 | 15 | 16 | 17 | 18 | 19 |
| 20 | 21 | 22 | 23 | 24 | 25 | 26 |
| 27 | 28 | 29 | 30 | 31 |   |   |

### AUGUST
| S | M | T | W | T | F | S |
|---|---|---|---|---|---|---|
|   |   |   |   |   | 1 | 2 |
| 3 | 4 | 5 | 6 | 7 | 8 | 9 |
| 10 | 11 | 12 | 13 | 14 | 15 | 16 |
| 17 | 18 | 19 | 20 | 21 | 22 | 23 |
| 24 | 25 | 26 | 27 | 28 | 29 | 30 |
| 31 |   |   |   |   |   |   |

### SEPTEMBER
| S | M | T | W | T | F | S |
|---|---|---|---|---|---|---|
|   | 1 | 2 | 3 | 4 | 5 | 6 |
| 7 | 8 | 9 | 10 | 11 | 12 | 13 |
| 14 | 15 | 16 | 17 | 18 | 19 | 20 |
| 21 | 22 | 23 | 24 | 25 | 26 | 27 |
| 28 | 29 | 30 |   |   |   |   |

### OCTOBER
| S | M | T | W | T | F | S |
|---|---|---|---|---|---|---|
|   |   |   | 1 | 2 | 3 | 4 |
| 5 | 6 | 7 | 8 | 9 | 10 | 11 |
| 12 | 13 | 14 | 15 | 16 | 17 | 18 |
| 19 | 20 | 21 | 22 | 23 | 24 | 25 |
| 26 | 27 | 28 | 29 | 30 | 31 |   |

### NOVEMBER
| S | M | T | W | T | F | S |
|---|---|---|---|---|---|---|
|   |   |   |   |   |   | 1 |
| 2 | 3 | 4 | 5 | 6 | 7 | 8 |
| 9 | 10 | 11 | 12 | 13 | 14 | 15 |
| 16 | 17 | 18 | 19 | 20 | 21 | 22 |
| 23 | 24 | 25 | 26 | 27 | 28 | 29 |
| 30 |   |   |   |   |   |   |

### DECEMBER
| S | M | T | W | T | F | S |
|---|---|---|---|---|---|---|
|   | 1 | 2 | 3 | 4 | 5 | 6 |
| 7 | 8 | 9 | 10 | 11 | 12 | 13 |
| 14 | 15 | 16 | 17 | 18 | 19 | 20 |
| 21 | 22 | 23 | 24 | 25 | 26 | 27 |
| 28 | 29 | 30 | 31 |   |   |   |

# E

**1789 1795 1801 1807 1818 1829 1835**
**1846 1857 1863 1874 1885 1891 1903**

## JANUARY

| S | M | T | W | T | F | S |
|---|---|---|---|---|---|---|
|   |   |   |   | 1 | 2 | 3 |
| 4 | 5 | 6 | 7 | 8 | 9 | 10 |
| 11 | 12 | 13 | 14 | 15 | 16 | 17 |
| 18 | 19 | 20 | 21 | 22 | 23 | 24 |
| 25 | 26 | 27 | 28 | 29 | 30 | 31 |

## FEBRUARY

| S | M | T | W | T | F | S |
|---|---|---|---|---|---|---|
| 1 | 2 | 3 | 4 | 5 | 6 | 7 |
| 8 | 9 | 10 | 11 | 12 | 13 | 14 |
| 15 | 16 | 17 | 18 | 19 | 20 | 21 |
| 22 | 23 | 24 | 25 | 26 | 27 | 28 |

## MARCH

| S | M | T | W | T | F | S |
|---|---|---|---|---|---|---|
| 1 | 2 | 3 | 4 | 5 | 6 | 7 |
| 8 | 9 | 10 | 11 | 12 | 13 | 14 |
| 15 | 16 | 17 | 18 | 19 | 20 | 21 |
| 22 | 23 | 24 | 25 | 26 | 27 | 28 |
| 29 | 30 | 31 |   |   |   |   |

## APRIL

| S | M | T | W | T | F | S |
|---|---|---|---|---|---|---|
|   |   |   | 1 | 2 | 3 | 4 |
| 5 | 6 | 7 | 8 | 9 | 10 | 11 |
| 12 | 13 | 14 | 15 | 16 | 17 | 18 |
| 19 | 20 | 21 | 22 | 23 | 24 | 25 |
| 26 | 27 | 28 | 29 | 30 |   |   |

## MAY

| S | M | T | W | T | F | S |
|---|---|---|---|---|---|---|
|   |   |   |   |   | 1 | 2 |
| 3 | 4 | 5 | 6 | 7 | 8 | 9 |
| 10 | 11 | 12 | 13 | 14 | 15 | 16 |
| 17 | 18 | 19 | 20 | 21 | 22 | 23 |
| 24 | 25 | 26 | 27 | 28 | 29 | 30 |
| 31 |   |   |   |   |   |   |

## JUNE

| S | M | T | W | T | F | S |
|---|---|---|---|---|---|---|
|   | 1 | 2 | 3 | 4 | 5 | 6 |
| 7 | 8 | 9 | 10 | 11 | 12 | 13 |
| 14 | 15 | 16 | 17 | 18 | 19 | 20 |
| 21 | 22 | 23 | 24 | 25 | 26 | 27 |
| 28 | 29 | 30 |   |   |   |   |

**1914   1925   1931   1942   1953   1959   1970**
**1981   1987   1998   2009   2015   2026   2037**
**2043**

# E

## JULY
| S | M | T | W | T | F | S |
|---|---|---|---|---|---|---|
|   |   | 1 | 2 | 3 | 4 |   |
| 5 | 6 | 7 | 8 | 9 | 10 | 11 |
| 12 | 13 | 14 | 15 | 16 | 17 | 18 |
| 19 | 20 | 21 | 22 | 23 | 24 | 25 |
| 26 | 27 | 28 | 29 | 30 | 31 |   |

## AUGUST
| S | M | T | W | T | F | S |
|---|---|---|---|---|---|---|
|   |   |   |   |   |   | 1 |
| 2 | 3 | 4 | 5 | 6 | 7 | 8 |
| 9 | 10 | 11 | 12 | 13 | 14 | 15 |
| 16 | 17 | 18 | 19 | 20 | 21 | 22 |
| 23 | 24 | 25 | 26 | 27 | 28 | 29 |
| 30 | 31 |   |   |   |   |   |

## SEPTEMBER
| S | M | T | W | T | F | S |
|---|---|---|---|---|---|---|
|   |   | 1 | 2 | 3 | 4 | 5 |
| 6 | 7 | 8 | 9 | 10 | 11 | 12 |
| 13 | 14 | 15 | 16 | 17 | 18 | 19 |
| 20 | 21 | 22 | 23 | 24 | 25 | 26 |
| 27 | 28 | 29 | 30 |   |   |   |

## OCTOBER
| S | M | T | W | T | F | S |
|---|---|---|---|---|---|---|
|   |   |   |   |   | 1 | 2 |
| 4 | 5 | 6 | 7 | 8 | 9 | 10 |
| 11 | 12 | 13 | 14 | 15 | 16 | 17 |
| 18 | 19 | 20 | 21 | 22 | 23 | 24 |
| 25 | 26 | 27 | 28 | 29 | 30 | 31 |

## NOVEMBER
| S | M | T | W | T | F | S |
|---|---|---|---|---|---|---|
| 1 | 2 | 3 | 4 | 5 | 6 | 7 |
| 8 | 9 | 10 | 11 | 12 | 13 | 14 |
| 15 | 16 | 17 | 18 | 19 | 20 | 21 |
| 22 | 23 | 24 | 25 | 26 | 27 | 28 |
| 29 | 30 |   |   |   |   |   |

## DECEMBER
| S | M | T | W | T | F | S |
|---|---|---|---|---|---|---|
|   |   | 1 | 2 | 3 | 4 | 5 |
| 6 | 7 | 8 | 9 | 10 | 11 | 12 |
| 13 | 14 | 15 | 16 | 17 | 18 | 19 |
| 20 | 21 | 22 | 23 | 24 | 25 | 26 |
| 27 | 28 | 29 | 30 | 31 |   |   |

**F** *1790  1802  1813  1819  1830  1841  1847*
*1858  1869  1875  1886  1897  1909  1915*

**JANUARY**

| S | M | T | W | T | F | S |
|---|---|---|---|---|---|---|
|   |   |   |   |   | 1 | 2 |
| 3 | 4 | 5 | 6 | 7 | 8 | 9 |
| 10 | 11 | 12 | 13 | 14 | 15 | 16 |
| 17 | 18 | 19 | 20 | 21 | 22 | 23 |
| 24 | 25 | 26 | 27 | 28 | 29 | 30 |
| 31 |   |   |   |   |   |   |

**FEBRUARY**

| S | M | T | W | T | F | S |
|---|---|---|---|---|---|---|
|   | 1 | 2 | 3 | 4 | 5 | 6 |
| 7 | 8 | 9 | 10 | 11 | 12 | 13 |
| 14 | 15 | 16 | 17 | 18 | 19 | 20 |
| 21 | 22 | 23 | 24 | 25 | 26 | 27 |
| 28 |   |   |   |   |   |   |

**MARCH**

| S | M | T | W | T | F | S |
|---|---|---|---|---|---|---|
|   | 1 | 2 | 3 | 4 | 5 | 6 |
| 7 | 8 | 9 | 10 | 11 | 12 | 13 |
| 14 | 15 | 16 | 17 | 18 | 19 | 20 |
| 21 | 22 | 23 | 24 | 25 | 26 | 27 |
| 28 | 29 | 30 | 31 |   |   |   |

**APRIL**

| S | M | T | W | T | F | S |
|---|---|---|---|---|---|---|
|   |   |   |   | 1 | 2 | 3 |
| 4 | 5 | 6 | 7 | 8 | 9 | 10 |
| 11 | 12 | 13 | 14 | 15 | 16 | 17 |
| 18 | 19 | 20 | 21 | 22 | 23 | 24 |
| 25 | 26 | 27 | 28 | 29 | 30 |   |

**MAY**

| S | M | T | W | T | F | S |
|---|---|---|---|---|---|---|
|   |   |   |   |   |   | 1 |
| 2 | 3 | 4 | 5 | 6 | 7 | 8 |
| 9 | 10 | 11 | 12 | 13 | 14 | 15 |
| 16 | 17 | 18 | 19 | 20 | 21 | 22 |
| 23 | 24 | 25 | 26 | 27 | 28 | 29 |
| 30 | 31 |   |   |   |   |   |

**JUNE**

| S | M | T | W | T | F | S |
|---|---|---|---|---|---|---|
|   |   | 1 | 2 | 3 | 4 | 5 |
| 6 | 7 | 8 | 9 | 10 | 11 | 12 |
| 13 | 14 | 15 | 16 | 17 | 18 | 19 |
| 20 | 21 | 22 | 23 | 24 | 25 | 26 |
| 27 | 28 | 29 | 30 |   |   |   |

**1926  1937  1943  1954  1965  1971  1982**
**1993  1999  2010  2021  2027  2038**     **F**

**JULY**

| S | M | T | W | T | F | S |
|---|---|---|---|---|---|---|
|   |   |   |   | 1 | 2 | 3 |
| 4 | 5 | 6 | 7 | 8 | 9 | 10 |
| 11 | 12 | 13 | 14 | 15 | 16 | 17 |
| 18 | 19 | 20 | 21 | 22 | 23 | 24 |
| 25 | 26 | 27 | 28 | 29 | 30 | 31 |

**AUGUST**

| S | M | T | W | T | F | S |
|---|---|---|---|---|---|---|
| 1 | 2 | 3 | 4 | 5 | 6 | 7 |
| 8 | 9 | 10 | 11 | 12 | 13 | 14 |
| 15 | 16 | 17 | 18 | 19 | 20 | 21 |
| 22 | 23 | 24 | 25 | 26 | 27 | 28 |
| 29 | 30 | 31 |   |   |   |   |

**SEPTEMBER**

| S | M | T | W | T | F | S |
|---|---|---|---|---|---|---|
|   |   |   | 1 | 2 | 3 | 4 |
| 5 | 6 | 7 | 8 | 9 | 10 | 11 |
| 12 | 13 | 14 | 15 | 16 | 17 | 18 |
| 19 | 20 | 21 | 22 | 23 | 24 | 25 |
| 26 | 27 | 28 | 29 | 30 |   |   |

**OCTOBER**

| S | M | T | W | T | F | S |
|---|---|---|---|---|---|---|
|   |   |   |   |   | 1 | 2 |
| 3 | 4 | 5 | 6 | 7 | 8 | 9 |
| 10 | 11 | 12 | 13 | 14 | 15 | 16 |
| 17 | 18 | 19 | 20 | 21 | 22 | 23 |
| 24 | 25 | 26 | 27 | 28 | 29 | 30 |
| 31 |   |   |   |   |   |   |

**NOVEMBER**

| S | M | T | W | T | F | S |
|---|---|---|---|---|---|---|
|   | 1 | 2 | 3 | 4 | 5 | 6 |
| 7 | 8 | 9 | 10 | 11 | 12 | 13 |
| 14 | 15 | 16 | 17 | 18 | 19 | 20 |
| 21 | 22 | 23 | 24 | 25 | 26 | 27 |
| 28 | 29 | 30 |   |   |   |   |

**DECEMBER**

| S | M | T | W | T | F | S |
|---|---|---|---|---|---|---|
|   |   |   | 1 | 2 | 3 | 4 |
| 5 | 6 | 7 | 8 | 9 | 10 | 11 |
| 12 | 13 | 14 | 15 | 16 | 17 | 18 |
| 19 | 20 | 21 | 22 | 23 | 24 | 25 |
| 26 | 27 | 28 | 29 | 30 | 31 |   |

# G
1785 1791 1803 1814 1825 1831 1842
1853 1859 1870 1881 1887 1898 1910

## JANUARY
| S | M | T | W | T | F | S |
|---|---|---|---|---|---|---|
|   |   |   |   |   |   | 1 |
| 2 | 3 | 4 | 5 | 6 | 7 | 8 |
| 9 | 10 | 11 | 12 | 13 | 14 | 15 |
| 16 | 17 | 18 | 19 | 20 | 21 | 22 |
| 23 | 24 | 25 | 26 | 27 | 28 | 29 |
| 30 | 31 |   |   |   |   |   |

## FEBRUARY
| S | M | T | W | T | F | S |
|---|---|---|---|---|---|---|
|   |   | 1 | 2 | 3 | 4 | 5 |
| 6 | 7 | 8 | 9 | 10 | 11 | 12 |
| 13 | 14 | 15 | 16 | 17 | 18 | 19 |
| 20 | 21 | 22 | 23 | 24 | 25 | 26 |
| 27 | 28 |   |   |   |   |   |

## MARCH
| S | M | T | W | T | F | S |
|---|---|---|---|---|---|---|
|   |   | 1 | 2 | 3 | 4 | 5 |
| 6 | 7 | 8 | 9 | 10 | 11 | 12 |
| 13 | 14 | 15 | 16 | 17 | 18 | 19 |
| 20 | 21 | 22 | 23 | 24 | 25 | 26 |
| 27 | 28 | 29 | 30 | 31 |   |   |

## APRIL
| S | M | T | W | T | F | S |
|---|---|---|---|---|---|---|
|   |   |   |   |   | 1 | 2 |
| 3 | 4 | 5 | 6 | 7 | 8 | 9 |
| 10 | 11 | 12 | 13 | 14 | 15 | 16 |
| 17 | 18 | 19 | 20 | 21 | 22 | 23 |
| 24 | 25 | 26 | 27 | 28 | 29 | 30 |

## MAY
| S | M | T | W | T | F | S |
|---|---|---|---|---|---|---|
| 1 | 2 | 3 | 4 | 5 | 6 | 7 |
| 8 | 9 | 10 | 11 | 12 | 13 | 14 |
| 15 | 16 | 17 | 18 | 19 | 20 | 21 |
| 22 | 23 | 24 | 25 | 26 | 27 | 28 |
| 29 | 30 | 31 |   |   |   |   |

## JUNE
| S | M | T | W | T | F | S |
|---|---|---|---|---|---|---|
|   |   |   | 1 | 2 | 3 | 4 |
| 5 | 6 | 7 | 8 | 9 | 10 | 11 |
| 12 | 13 | 14 | 15 | 16 | 17 | 18 |
| 19 | 20 | 21 | 22 | 23 | 24 | 25 |
| 26 | 27 | 28 | 29 | 30 |   |   |

**1921 1927 1938 1949 1955 1966 1977 G**
**1983 1994 2005 2011 2022 2033 2039**

**JULY**

| S | M | T | W | T | F | S |
|---|---|---|---|---|---|---|
|   |   |   |   |   | 1 | 2 |
| 3 | 4 | 5 | 6 | 7 | 8 | 9 |
| 10 | 11 | 12 | 13 | 14 | 15 | 16 |
| 17 | 18 | 19 | 20 | 21 | 22 | 23 |
| 24 | 25 | 26 | 27 | 28 | 29 | 30 |
| 31 |   |   |   |   |   |   |

**AUGUST**

| S | M | T | W | T | F | S |
|---|---|---|---|---|---|---|
|   |   | 1 | 2 | 3 | 4 | 5 | 6 |
| 7 | 8 | 9 | 10 | 11 | 12 | 13 |
| 14 | 15 | 16 | 17 | 18 | 19 | 20 |
| 21 | 22 | 23 | 24 | 25 | 26 | 27 |
| 28 | 29 | 30 | 31 |   |   |   |

**SEPTEMBER**

| S | M | T | W | T | F | S |
|---|---|---|---|---|---|---|
|   |   |   |   | 1 | 2 | 3 |
| 4 | 5 | 6 | 7 | 8 | 9 | 10 |
| 11 | 12 | 13 | 14 | 15 | 16 | 17 |
| 18 | 19 | 20 | 21 | 22 | 23 | 24 |
| 25 | 26 | 27 | 28 | 29 | 30 |   |

**OCTOBER**

| S | M | T | W | T | F | S |
|---|---|---|---|---|---|---|
|   |   |   |   |   |   | 1 |
| 2 | 3 | 4 | 5 | 6 | 7 | 8 |
| 9 | 10 | 11 | 12 | 13 | 14 | 15 |
| 16 | 17 | 18 | 19 | 20 | 21 | 22 |
| 23 | 24 | 25 | 26 | 27 | 28 | 29 |
| 30 | 31 |   |   |   |   |   |

**NOVEMBER**

| S | M | T | W | T | F | S |
|---|---|---|---|---|---|---|
|   |   | 1 | 2 | 3 | 4 | 5 |
| 6 | 7 | 8 | 9 | 10 | 11 | 12 |
| 13 | 14 | 15 | 16 | 17 | 18 | 19 |
| 20 | 21 | 22 | 23 | 24 | 25 | 26 |
| 27 | 28 | 29 | 30 |   |   |   |

**DECEMBER**

| S | M | T | W | T | F | S |
|---|---|---|---|---|---|---|
|   |   |   |   | 1 | 2 | 3 |
| 4 | 5 | 6 | 7 | 8 | 9 | 10 |
| 11 | 12 | 13 | 14 | 15 | 16 | 17 |
| 18 | 19 | 20 | 21 | 22 | 23 | 24 |
| 25 | 26 | 27 | 28 | 29 | 30 | 31 |

# H
### 1792 1804 1832 1860 1888
### 1928 1956 1984 2012 2040

## JANUARY
| S | M | T | W | T | F | S |
|---|---|---|---|---|---|---|
| 1 | 2 | 3 | 4 | 5 | 6 | 7 |
| 8 | 9 | 10 | 11 | 12 | 13 | 14 |
| 15 | 16 | 17 | 18 | 19 | 20 | 21 |
| 22 | 23 | 24 | 25 | 26 | 27 | 28 |
| 29 | 30 | 31 | | | | |

## FEBRUARY
| S | M | T | W | T | F | S |
|---|---|---|---|---|---|---|
| | | | | 1 | 2 | 3 | 4 |
| 5 | 6 | 7 | 8 | 9 | 10 | 11 |
| 12 | 13 | 14 | 15 | 16 | 17 | 18 |
| 19 | 20 | 21 | 22 | 23 | 24 | 25 |
| 26 | 27 | 28 | 29 | | | |

## MARCH
| S | M | T | W | T | F | S |
|---|---|---|---|---|---|---|
| | | | | 1 | 2 | 3 |
| 4 | 5 | 6 | 7 | 8 | 9 | 10 |
| 11 | 12 | 13 | 14 | 15 | 16 | 17 |
| 18 | 19 | 20 | 21 | 22 | 23 | 24 |
| 25 | 26 | 27 | 28 | 29 | 30 | 31 |

## APRIL
| S | M | T | W | T | F | S |
|---|---|---|---|---|---|---|
| 1 | 2 | 3 | 4 | 5 | 6 | 7 |
| 8 | 9 | 10 | 11 | 12 | 13 | 14 |
| 15 | 16 | 17 | 18 | 19 | 20 | 21 |
| 22 | 23 | 24 | 25 | 26 | 27 | 28 |
| 29 | 30 | | | | | |

## MAY
| S | M | T | W | T | F | S |
|---|---|---|---|---|---|---|
| | | 1 | 2 | 3 | 4 | 5 |
| 6 | 7 | 8 | 9 | 10 | 11 | 12 |
| 13 | 14 | 15 | 16 | 17 | 18 | 19 |
| 20 | 21 | 22 | 23 | 24 | 25 | 26 |
| 27 | 28 | 29 | 30 | 31 | | |

## JUNE
| S | M | T | W | T | F | S |
|---|---|---|---|---|---|---|
| | | | | | 1 | 2 |
| 3 | 4 | 5 | 6 | 7 | 8 | 9 |
| 10 | 11 | 12 | 13 | 14 | 15 | 16 |
| 17 | 18 | 19 | 20 | 21 | 22 | 23 |
| 24 | 25 | 26 | 27 | 28 | 29 | 30 |

# H

**JULY**

| S | M | T | W | T | F | S |
|---|---|---|---|---|---|---|
|  | 1 | 2 | 3 | 4 | 5 | 6 | 7 |
| 8 | 9 | 10 | 11 | 12 | 13 | 14 |
| 15 | 16 | 17 | 18 | 19 | 20 | 21 |
| 22 | 23 | 24 | 25 | 26 | 27 | 28 |
| 29 | 30 | 31 |  |  |  |  |

**AUGUST**

| S | M | T | W | T | F | S |
|---|---|---|---|---|---|---|
|  |  |  |  | 1 | 2 | 3 | 4 |
| 5 | 6 | 7 | 8 | 9 | 10 | 11 |
| 12 | 13 | 14 | 15 | 16 | 17 | 18 |
| 19 | 20 | 21 | 22 | 23 | 24 | 25 |
| 26 | 27 | 28 | 29 | 30 | 31 |  |

**SEPTEMBER**

| S | M | T | W | T | F | S |
|---|---|---|---|---|---|---|
|  |  |  |  |  |  | 1 |
| 2 | 3 | 4 | 5 | 6 | 7 | 8 |
| 9 | 10 | 11 | 12 | 13 | 14 | 15 |
| 16 | 17 | 18 | 19 | 20 | 21 | 22 |
| 23 | 24 | 25 | 26 | 27 | 28 | 29 |
| 30 |  |  |  |  |  |  |

**OCTOBER**

| S | M | T | W | T | F | S |
|---|---|---|---|---|---|---|
|  | 1 | 2 | 3 | 4 | 5 | 6 |
| 7 | 8 | 9 | 10 | 11 | 12 | 13 |
| 14 | 15 | 16 | 17 | 18 | 19 | 20 |
| 21 | 22 | 23 | 24 | 25 | 26 | 27 |
| 28 | 29 | 30 | 31 |  |  |  |

**NOVEMBER**

| S | M | T | W | T | F | S |
|---|---|---|---|---|---|---|
|  |  |  |  | 1 | 2 | 3 |
| 4 | 5 | 6 | 7 | 8 | 9 | 10 |
| 11 | 12 | 13 | 14 | 15 | 16 | 17 |
| 18 | 19 | 20 | 21 | 22 | 23 | 24 |
| 25 | 26 | 27 | 28 | 29 | 30 |  |

**DECEMBER**

| S | M | T | W | T | F | S |
|---|---|---|---|---|---|---|
|  |  |  |  |  |  | 1 |
| 2 | 3 | 4 | 5 | 6 | 7 | 8 |
| 9 | 10 | 11 | 12 | 13 | 14 | 15 |
| 16 | 17 | 18 | 19 | 20 | 21 | 22 |
| 23 | 24 | 25 | 26 | 27 | 28 | 29 |
| 30 | 31 |  |  |  |  |  |

**I** 1816 1844 1872 1912
1940 1968 1996 2024

## JANUARY
| S | M | T | W | T | F | S |
|---|---|---|---|---|---|---|
|   |   | 1 | 2 | 3 | 4 | 5 | 6 |
| 7 | 8 | 9 | 10 | 11 | 12 | 13 |
| 14 | 15 | 16 | 17 | 18 | 19 | 20 |
| 21 | 22 | 23 | 24 | 25 | 26 | 27 |
| 28 | 29 | 30 | 31 |   |   |   |

## FEBRUARY
| S | M | T | W | T | F | S |
|---|---|---|---|---|---|---|
|   |   |   |   | 1 | 2 | 3 |
| 4 | 5 | 6 | 7 | 8 | 9 | 10 |
| 11 | 12 | 13 | 14 | 15 | 16 | 17 |
| 18 | 19 | 20 | 21 | 22 | 23 | 24 |
| 25 | 26 | 27 | 28 | 29 |   |   |

## MARCH
| S | M | T | W | T | F | S |
|---|---|---|---|---|---|---|
|   |   |   |   |   | 1 | 2 |
| 3 | 4 | 5 | 6 | 7 | 8 | 9 |
| 10 | 11 | 12 | 13 | 14 | 15 | 16 |
| 17 | 18 | 19 | 20 | 21 | 22 | 23 |
| 24 | 25 | 26 | 27 | 28 | 29 | 30 |
| 31 |   |   |   |   |   |   |

## APRIL
| S | M | T | W | T | F | S |
|---|---|---|---|---|---|---|
|   | 1 | 2 | 3 | 4 | 5 | 6 |
| 7 | 8 | 9 | 10 | 11 | 12 | 13 |
| 14 | 15 | 16 | 17 | 18 | 19 | 20 |
| 21 | 22 | 23 | 24 | 25 | 26 | 27 |
| 28 | 29 | 30 |   |   |   |   |

## MAY
| S | M | T | W | T | F | S |
|---|---|---|---|---|---|---|
|   |   |   | 1 | 2 | 3 | 4 |
| 5 | 6 | 7 | 8 | 9 | 10 | 11 |
| 12 | 13 | 14 | 15 | 16 | 17 | 18 |
| 19 | 20 | 21 | 22 | 23 | 24 | 25 |
| 26 | 27 | 28 | 29 | 30 | 31 |   |

## JUNE
| S | M | T | W | T | F | S |
|---|---|---|---|---|---|---|
|   |   |   |   |   |   | 1 |
| 2 | 3 | 4 | 5 | 6 | 7 | 8 |
| 9 | 10 | 11 | 12 | 13 | 14 | 15 |
| 16 | 17 | 18 | 19 | 20 | 21 | 22 |
| 23 | 24 | 25 | 26 | 27 | 28 | 29 |
| 30 |   |   |   |   |   |   |

# I

## JULY

| S | M | T | W | T | F | S |
|---|---|---|---|---|---|---|
|  | 1 | 2 | 3 | 4 | 5 | 6 |
| 7 | 8 | 9 | 10 | 11 | 12 | 13 |
| 14 | 15 | 16 | 17 | 18 | 19 | 20 |
| 21 | 22 | 23 | 24 | 25 | 26 | 27 |
| 28 | 29 | 30 | 31 |  |  |  |

## AUGUST

| S | M | T | W | T | F | S |
|---|---|---|---|---|---|---|
|  |  |  |  |  | 1 | 2 | 3 |
| 4 | 5 | 6 | 7 | 8 | 9 | 10 |
| 11 | 12 | 13 | 14 | 15 | 16 | 17 |
| 18 | 19 | 20 | 21 | 22 | 23 | 24 |
| 25 | 26 | 27 | 28 | 29 | 30 | 31 |

## SEPTEMBER

| S | M | T | W | T | F | S |
|---|---|---|---|---|---|---|
| 1 | 2 | 3 | 4 | 5 | 6 | 7 |
| 8 | 9 | 10 | 11 | 12 | 13 | 14 |
| 15 | 16 | 17 | 18 | 19 | 20 | 21 |
| 22 | 23 | 24 | 25 | 26 | 27 | 28 |
| 29 | 30 |  |  |  |  |  |

## OCTOBER

| S | M | T | W | T | F | S |
|---|---|---|---|---|---|---|
|  |  | 1 | 2 | 3 | 4 | 5 |
| 6 | 7 | 8 | 9 | 10 | 11 | 12 |
| 13 | 14 | 15 | 16 | 17 | 18 | 19 |
| 20 | 21 | 22 | 23 | 24 | 25 | 26 |
| 27 | 28 | 29 | 30 | 31 |  |  |

## NOVEMBER

| S | M | T | W | T | F | S |
|---|---|---|---|---|---|---|
|  |  |  |  |  | 1 | 2 |
| 3 | 4 | 5 | 6 | 7 | 8 | 9 |
| 10 | 11 | 12 | 13 | 14 | 15 | 16 |
| 17 | 18 | 19 | 20 | 21 | 22 | 23 |
| 24 | 25 | 26 | 27 | 28 | 29 | 30 |

## DECEMBER

| S | M | T | W | T | F | S |
|---|---|---|---|---|---|---|
| 1 | 2 | 3 | 4 | 5 | 6 | 7 |
| 8 | 9 | 10 | 11 | 12 | 13 | 14 |
| 15 | 16 | 17 | 18 | 19 | 20 | 21 |
| 22 | 23 | 24 | 25 | 26 | 27 | 28 |
| 29 | 30 | 31 |  |  |  |  |

# J 1788 1828 1856 1884 1924
1952 1980 2008 2036

**JANUARY**

| S | M | T | W | T | F | S |
|---|---|---|---|---|---|---|
|   |   | 1 | 2 | 3 | 4 | 5 |
| 6 | 7 | 8 | 9 | 10 | 11 | 12 |
| 13 | 14 | 15 | 16 | 17 | 18 | 19 |
| 20 | 21 | 22 | 23 | 24 | 25 | 26 |
| 27 | 28 | 29 | 30 | 31 |   |   |

**FEBRUARY**

| S | M | T | W | T | F | S |
|---|---|---|---|---|---|---|
|   |   |   |   |   | 1 | 2 |
| 3 | 4 | 5 | 6 | 7 | 8 | 9 |
| 10 | 11 | 12 | 13 | 14 | 15 | 16 |
| 17 | 18 | 19 | 20 | 21 | 22 | 23 |
| 24 | 25 | 26 | 27 | 28 | 29 |   |

**MARCH**

| S | M | T | W | T | F | S |
|---|---|---|---|---|---|---|
|   |   |   |   |   |   | 1 |
| 2 | 3 | 4 | 5 | 6 | 7 | 8 |
| 9 | 10 | 11 | 12 | 13 | 14 | 15 |
| 16 | 17 | 18 | 19 | 20 | 21 | 22 |
| 23 | 24 | 25 | 26 | 27 | 28 | 29 |
| 30 | 31 |   |   |   |   |   |

**APRIL**

| S | M | T | W | T | F | S |
|---|---|---|---|---|---|---|
|   |   | 1 | 2 | 3 | 4 | 5 |
| 6 | 7 | 8 | 9 | 10 | 11 | 12 |
| 13 | 14 | 15 | 16 | 17 | 18 | 19 |
| 20 | 21 | 22 | 23 | 24 | 25 | 26 |
| 27 | 28 | 29 | 30 |   |   |   |

**MAY**

| S | M | T | W | T | F | S |
|---|---|---|---|---|---|---|
|   |   |   |   | 1 | 2 | 3 |
| 4 | 5 | 6 | 7 | 8 | 9 | 10 |
| 11 | 12 | 13 | 14 | 15 | 16 | 17 |
| 18 | 19 | 20 | 21 | 22 | 23 | 24 |
| 25 | 26 | 27 | 28 | 29 | 30 | 31 |

**JUNE**

| S | M | T | W | T | F | S |
|---|---|---|---|---|---|---|
| 1 | 2 | 3 | 4 | 5 | 6 | 7 |
| 8 | 9 | 10 | 11 | 12 | 13 | 14 |
| 15 | 16 | 17 | 18 | 19 | 20 | 21 |
| 22 | 23 | 24 | 25 | 26 | 27 | 28 |
| 29 | 30 |   |   |   |   |   |

# J

## JULY
| S | M | T | W | T | F | S |
|---|---|---|---|---|---|---|
|  |  | 1 | 2 | 3 | 4 | 5 |
| 6 | 7 | 8 | 9 | 10 | 11 | 12 |
| 13 | 14 | 15 | 16 | 17 | 18 | 19 |
| 20 | 21 | 22 | 23 | 24 | 25 | 26 |
| 27 | 28 | 29 | 30 | 31 |  |  |

## AUGUST
| S | M | T | W | T | F | S |
|---|---|---|---|---|---|---|
|  |  |  |  |  | 1 | 2 |
| 3 | 4 | 5 | 6 | 7 | 8 | 9 |
| 10 | 11 | 12 | 13 | 14 | 15 | 16 |
| 17 | 18 | 19 | 20 | 21 | 22 | 23 |
| 24 | 25 | 26 | 27 | 28 | 29 | 30 |
| 31 |  |  |  |  |  |  |

## SEPTEMBER
| S | M | T | W | T | F | S |
|---|---|---|---|---|---|---|
|  | 1 | 2 | 3 | 4 | 5 | 6 |
| 7 | 8 | 9 | 10 | 11 | 12 | 13 |
| 14 | 15 | 16 | 17 | 18 | 19 | 20 |
| 21 | 22 | 23 | 24 | 25 | 26 | 27 |
| 28 | 29 | 30 |  |  |  |  |

## OCTOBER
| S | M | T | W | T | F | S |
|---|---|---|---|---|---|---|
|  |  |  | 1 | 2 | 3 | 4 |
| 5 | 6 | 7 | 8 | 9 | 10 | 11 |
| 12 | 13 | 14 | 15 | 16 | 17 | 18 |
| 19 | 20 | 21 | 22 | 23 | 24 | 25 |
| 26 | 27 | 28 | 29 | 30 | 31 |  |

## NOVEMBER
| S | M | T | W | T | F | S |
|---|---|---|---|---|---|---|
|  |  |  |  |  |  | 1 |
| 2 | 3 | 4 | 5 | 6 | 7 | 8 |
| 9 | 10 | 11 | 12 | 13 | 14 | 15 |
| 16 | 17 | 18 | 19 | 20 | 21 | 22 |
| 23 | 24 | 25 | 26 | 27 | 28 | 29 |
| 30 |  |  |  |  |  |  |

## DECEMBER
| S | M | T | W | T | F | S |
|---|---|---|---|---|---|---|
|  | 1 | 2 | 3 | 4 | 5 | 6 |
| 7 | 8 | 9 | 10 | 11 | 12 | 13 |
| 14 | 15 | 16 | 17 | 18 | 19 | 20 |
| 21 | 22 | 23 | 24 | 25 | 26 | 27 |
| 28 | 29 | 30 | 31 |  |  |  |

# K 1812 1840 1868 1896 1908
## 1936 1964 1992 2020

**JANUARY**

| S | M | T | W | T | F | S |
|---|---|---|---|---|---|---|
|   |   |   | 1 | 2 | 3 | 4 |
| 5 | 6 | 7 | 8 | 9 | 10 | 11 |
| 12 | 13 | 14 | 15 | 16 | 17 | 18 |
| 19 | 20 | 21 | 22 | 23 | 24 | 25 |
| 26 | 27 | 28 | 29 | 30 | 31 |   |

**FEBRUARY**

| S | M | T | W | T | F | S |
|---|---|---|---|---|---|---|
|   |   |   |   |   |   | 1 |
| 2 | 3 | 4 | 5 | 6 | 7 | 8 |
| 9 | 10 | 11 | 12 | 13 | 14 | 15 |
| 16 | 17 | 18 | 19 | 20 | 21 | 22 |
| 23 | 24 | 25 | 26 | 27 | 28 | 29 |

**MARCH**

| S | M | T | W | T | F | S |
|---|---|---|---|---|---|---|
| 1 | 2 | 3 | 4 | 5 | 6 | 7 |
| 8 | 9 | 10 | 11 | 12 | 13 | 14 |
| 15 | 16 | 17 | 18 | 19 | 20 | 21 |
| 22 | 23 | 24 | 25 | 26 | 27 | 28 |
| 29 | 30 | 31 |   |   |   |   |

**APRIL**

| S | M | T | W | T | F | S |
|---|---|---|---|---|---|---|
|   |   |   | 1 | 2 | 3 | 4 |
| 5 | 6 | 7 | 8 | 9 | 10 | 11 |
| 12 | 13 | 14 | 15 | 16 | 17 | 18 |
| 19 | 20 | 21 | 22 | 23 | 24 | 25 |
| 26 | 27 | 28 | 29 | 30 |   |   |

**MAY**

| S | M | T | W | T | F | S |
|---|---|---|---|---|---|---|
|   |   |   |   |   | 1 | 2 |
| 3 | 4 | 5 | 6 | 7 | 8 | 9 |
| 10 | 11 | 12 | 13 | 14 | 15 | 16 |
| 17 | 18 | 19 | 20 | 21 | 22 | 23 |
| 24 | 25 | 26 | 27 | 28 | 29 | 30 |
| 31 |   |   |   |   |   |   |

**JUNE**

| S | M | T | W | T | F | S |
|---|---|---|---|---|---|---|
|   | 1 | 2 | 3 | 4 | 5 | 6 |
| 7 | 8 | 9 | 10 | 11 | 12 | 13 |
| 14 | 15 | 16 | 17 | 18 | 19 | 20 |
| 21 | 22 | 23 | 24 | 25 | 26 | 27 |
| 28 | 29 | 30 |   |   |   |   |

# K

### JULY
| S | M | T | W | T | F | S |
|---|---|---|---|---|---|---|
| | | | 1 | 2 | 3 | 4 |
| 5 | 6 | 7 | 8 | 9 | 10 | 11 |
| 12 | 13 | 14 | 15 | 16 | 17 | 18 |
| 19 | 20 | 21 | 22 | 23 | 24 | 25 |
| 26 | 27 | 28 | 29 | 30 | 31 | |

### AUGUST
| S | M | T | W | T | F | S |
|---|---|---|---|---|---|---|
| | | | | | | 1 |
| 2 | 3 | 4 | 5 | 6 | 7 | 8 |
| 9 | 10 | 11 | 12 | 13 | 14 | 15 |
| 16 | 17 | 18 | 19 | 20 | 21 | 22 |
| 23 | 24 | 25 | 26 | 27 | 28 | 29 |
| 30 | 31 | | | | | |

### SEPTEMBER
| S | M | T | W | T | F | S |
|---|---|---|---|---|---|---|
| | | 1 | 2 | 3 | 4 | 5 |
| 6 | 7 | 8 | 9 | 10 | 11 | 12 |
| 13 | 14 | 15 | 16 | 1/ | 18 | 19 |
| 20 | 21 | 22 | 23 | 24 | 25 | 26 |
| 27 | 28 | 29 | 30 | | | |

### OCTOBER
| S | M | T | W | T | F | S |
|---|---|---|---|---|---|---|
| | | | | 1 | 2 | 3 |
| 4 | 5 | 6 | 7 | 8 | 9 | 10 |
| 11 | 12 | 13 | 14 | 15 | 16 | 17 |
| 18 | 19 | 20 | 21 | 22 | 23 | 24 |
| 25 | 26 | 27 | 28 | 29 | 30 | 31 |

### NOVEMBER
| S | M | T | W | T | F | S |
|---|---|---|---|---|---|---|
| 1 | 2 | 3 | 4 | 5 | 6 | 7 |
| 8 | 9 | 10 | 11 | 12 | 13 | 14 |
| 15 | 16 | 17 | 18 | 19 | 20 | 21 |
| 22 | 23 | 24 | 25 | 26 | 27 | 28 |
| 29 | 30 | | | | | |

### DECEMBER
| S | M | T | W | T | F | S |
|---|---|---|---|---|---|---|
| | | 1 | 2 | 3 | 4 | 5 |
| 6 | 7 | 8 | 9 | 10 | 11 | 12 |
| 13 | 14 | 15 | 16 | 17 | 18 | 19 |
| 20 | 21 | 22 | 23 | 24 | 25 | 26 |
| 27 | 28 | 29 | 30 | 31 | | |

# L  1784 1824 1852 1880 1920
## 1948 1976 2004 2032

**JANUARY**

| S | M | T | W | T | F | S |
|---|---|---|---|---|---|---|
|   |   |   |   | 1 | 2 | 3 |
| 4 | 5 | 6 | 7 | 8 | 9 | 10 |
| 11 | 12 | 13 | 14 | 15 | 16 | 17 |
| 18 | 19 | 20 | 21 | 22 | 23 | 24 |
| 25 | 26 | 27 | 28 | 29 | 30 | 31 |

**FEBRUARY**

| S | M | T | W | T | F | S |
|---|---|---|---|---|---|---|
| 1 | 2 | 3 | 4 | 5 | 6 | 7 |
| 8 | 9 | 10 | 11 | 12 | 13 | 14 |
| 15 | 16 | 17 | 18 | 19 | 20 | 21 |
| 22 | 23 | 24 | 25 | 26 | 27 | 28 |
| 29 |   |   |   |   |   |   |

**MARCH**

| S | M | T | W | T | F | S |
|---|---|---|---|---|---|---|
|   | 1 | 2 | 3 | 4 | 5 | 6 |
| 7 | 8 | 9 | 10 | 11 | 12 | 13 |
| 14 | 15 | 16 | 17 | 18 | 19 | 20 |
| 21 | 22 | 23 | 24 | 25 | 26 | 27 |
| 28 | 29 | 30 | 31 |   |   |   |

**APRIL**

| S | M | T | W | T | F | S |
|---|---|---|---|---|---|---|
|   |   |   |   | 1 | 2 | 3 |
| 4 | 5 | 6 | 7 | 8 | 9 | 10 |
| 11 | 12 | 13 | 14 | 15 | 16 | 17 |
| 18 | 19 | 20 | 21 | 22 | 23 | 24 |
| 25 | 26 | 27 | 28 | 29 | 30 |   |

**MAY**

| S | M | T | W | T | F | S |
|---|---|---|---|---|---|---|
|   |   |   |   |   |   | 1 |
| 2 | 3 | 4 | 5 | 6 | 7 | 8 |
| 9 | 10 | 11 | 12 | 13 | 14 | 15 |
| 16 | 17 | 18 | 19 | 20 | 21 | 22 |
| 23 | 24 | 25 | 26 | 27 | 28 | 29 |
| 30 | 31 |   |   |   |   |   |

**JUNE**

| S | M | T | W | T | F | S |
|---|---|---|---|---|---|---|
|   |   | 1 | 2 | 3 | 4 | 5 |
| 6 | 7 | 8 | 9 | 10 | 11 | 12 |
| 13 | 14 | 15 | 16 | 17 | 18 | 19 |
| 20 | 21 | 22 | 23 | 24 | 25 | 26 |
| 27 | 28 | 29 | 30 |   |   |   |

**L**

## JULY
| S | M | T | W | T | F | S |
|---|---|---|---|---|---|---|
|   |   |   |   | 1 | 2 | 3 |
| 4 | 5 | 6 | 7 | 8 | 9 | 10 |
| 11 | 12 | 13 | 14 | 15 | 16 | 17 |
| 18 | 19 | 20 | 21 | 22 | 23 | 24 |
| 25 | 26 | 27 | 28 | 29 | 30 | 31 |

## AUGUST
| S | M | T | W | T | F | S |
|---|---|---|---|---|---|---|
| 1 | 2 | 3 | 4 | 5 | 6 | 7 |
| 8 | 9 | 10 | 11 | 12 | 13 | 14 |
| 15 | 16 | 17 | 18 | 19 | 20 | 21 |
| 22 | 23 | 24 | 25 | 26 | 27 | 28 |
| 29 | 30 | 31 |   |   |   |   |

## SEPTEMBER
| S | M | T | W | T | F | S |
|---|---|---|---|---|---|---|
|   |   |   | 1 | 2 | 3 | 4 |
| 5 | 6 | 7 | 8 | 9 | 10 | 11 |
| 12 | 13 | 14 | 15 | 16 | 17 | 18 |
| 19 | 20 | 21 | 22 | 23 | 24 | 25 |
| 26 | 27 | 28 | 29 | 30 |   |   |

## OCTOBER
| S | M | T | W | T | F | S |
|---|---|---|---|---|---|---|
|   |   |   |   |   | 1 | 2 |
| 3 | 4 | 5 | 6 | 7 | 8 | 9 |
| 10 | 11 | 12 | 13 | 14 | 15 | 16 |
| 17 | 18 | 19 | 20 | 21 | 22 | 23 |
| 24 | 25 | 26 | 27 | 28 | 29 | 30 |
| 31 |   |   |   |   |   |   |

## NOVEMBER
| S | M | T | W | T | F | S |
|---|---|---|---|---|---|---|
|   | 1 | 2 | 3 | 4 | 5 | 6 |
| 7 | 8 | 9 | 10 | 11 | 12 | 13 |
| 14 | 15 | 16 | 17 | 18 | 19 | 20 |
| 21 | 22 | 23 | 24 | 25 | 26 | 27 |
| 28 | 29 | 30 |   |   |   |   |

## DECEMBER
| S | M | T | W | T | F | S |
|---|---|---|---|---|---|---|
|   |   |   | 1 | 2 | 3 | 4 |
| 5 | 6 | 7 | 8 | 9 | 10 | 11 |
| 12 | 13 | 14 | 15 | 16 | 17 | 18 |
| 19 | 20 | 21 | 22 | 23 | 24 | 25 |
| 26 | 27 | 28 | 29 | 30 | 31 |   |

**M** 1796 1808 1836 1864 1892 1904
1932 1960 1988 2016 2044

## JANUARY
| S | M | T | W | T | F | S |
|---|---|---|---|---|---|---|
|   |   |   |   |   | 1 | 2 |
| 3 | 4 | 5 | 6 | 7 | 8 | 9 |
| 10 | 11 | 12 | 13 | 14 | 15 | 16 |
| 17 | 18 | 19 | 20 | 21 | 22 | 23 |
| 24 | 25 | 26 | 27 | 28 | 29 | 30 |
| 31 |   |   |   |   |   |   |

## FEBRUARY
| S | M | T | W | T | F | S |
|---|---|---|---|---|---|---|
|   | 1 | 2 | 3 | 4 | 5 | 6 |
| 7 | 8 | 9 | 10 | 11 | 12 | 13 |
| 14 | 15 | 16 | 17 | 18 | 19 | 20 |
| 21 | 22 | 23 | 24 | 25 | 26 | 27 |
| 28 | 29 |   |   |   |   |   |

## MARCH
| S | M | T | W | T | F | S |
|---|---|---|---|---|---|---|
|   |   | 1 | 2 | 3 | 4 | 5 |
| 6 | 7 | 8 | 9 | 10 | 11 | 12 |
| 13 | 14 | 15 | 16 | 17 | 18 | 19 |
| 20 | 21 | 22 | 23 | 24 | 25 | 26 |
| 27 | 28 | 29 | 30 | 31 |   |   |

## APRIL
| S | M | T | W | T | F | S |
|---|---|---|---|---|---|---|
|   |   |   |   |   | 1 | 2 |
| 3 | 4 | 5 | 6 | 7 | 8 | 9 |
| 10 | 11 | 12 | 13 | 14 | 15 | 16 |
| 17 | 18 | 19 | 20 | 21 | 22 | 23 |
| 24 | 25 | 26 | 27 | 28 | 29 | 30 |

## MAY
| S | M | T | W | T | F | S |
|---|---|---|---|---|---|---|
| 1 | 2 | 3 | 4 | 5 | 6 | 7 |
| 8 | 9 | 10 | 11 | 12 | 13 | 14 |
| 15 | 16 | 17 | 18 | 19 | 20 | 21 |
| 22 | 23 | 24 | 25 | 26 | 27 | 28 |
| 29 | 30 | 31 |   |   |   |   |

## JUNE
| S | M | T | W | T | F | S |
|---|---|---|---|---|---|---|
|   |   |   | 1 | 2 | 3 | 4 |
| 5 | 6 | 7 | 8 | 9 | 10 | 11 |
| 12 | 13 | 14 | 15 | 16 | 17 | 18 |
| 19 | 20 | 21 | 22 | 23 | 24 | 25 |
| 26 | 27 | 28 | 29 | 30 |   |   |

# M

**JULY**

| S | M | T | W | T | F | S |
|---|---|---|---|---|---|---|
|   |   |   |   |   | 1 | 2 |
| 3 | 4 | 5 | 6 | 7 | 8 | 9 |
| 10 | 11 | 12 | 13 | 14 | 15 | 16 |
| 17 | 18 | 19 | 20 | 21 | 22 | 23 |
| 24 | 25 | 26 | 27 | 28 | 29 | 30 |
| 31 |   |   |   |   |   |   |

**AUGUST**

| S | M | T | W | T | F | S |
|---|---|---|---|---|---|---|
|   | 1 | 2 | 3 | 4 | 5 | 6 |
| 7 | 8 | 9 | 10 | 11 | 12 | 13 |
| 14 | 15 | 16 | 17 | 18 | 19 | 20 |
| 21 | 22 | 23 | 24 | 25 | 26 | 27 |
| 28 | 29 | 30 | 31 |   |   |   |

**SEPTEMBER**

| S | M | T | W | T | F | S |
|---|---|---|---|---|---|---|
|   |   |   |   | 1 | 2 | 3 |
| 4 | 5 | 6 | 7 | 8 | 9 | 10 |
| 11 | 12 | 13 | 14 | 15 | 16 | 17 |
| 18 | 19 | 20 | 21 | 22 | 23 | 24 |
| 25 | 26 | 27 | 28 | 29 | 30 |   |

**OCTOBER**

| S | M | T | W | T | F | S |
|---|---|---|---|---|---|---|
|   |   |   |   |   |   | 1 |
| 2 | 3 | 4 | 5 | 6 | 7 | 8 |
| 9 | 10 | 11 | 12 | 13 | 14 | 15 |
| 16 | 17 | 18 | 19 | 20 | 21 | 22 |
| 23 | 24 | 25 | 26 | 27 | 28 | 29 |
| 30 | 31 |   |   |   |   |   |

**NOVEMBER**

| S | M | T | W | T | F | S |
|---|---|---|---|---|---|---|
|   |   | 1 | 2 | 3 | 4 | 5 |
| 6 | 7 | 8 | 9 | 10 | 11 | 12 |
| 13 | 14 | 15 | 16 | 17 | 18 | 19 |
| 20 | 21 | 22 | 23 | 24 | 25 | 26 |
| 27 | 28 | 29 | 30 |   |   |   |

**DECEMBER**

| S | M | T | W | T | F | S |
|---|---|---|---|---|---|---|
|   |   |   |   | 1 | 2 | 3 |
| 4 | 5 | 6 | 7 | 8 | 9 | 10 |
| 11 | 12 | 13 | 14 | 15 | 16 | 17 |
| 18 | 19 | 20 | 21 | 22 | 23 | 24 |
| 25 | 26 | 27 | 28 | 29 | 30 | 31 |

**N** 1780 1820 1848 1876 1916
1944 1972 2000 2028

### JANUARY

| S | M | T | W | T | F | S |
|---|---|---|---|---|---|---|
|   |   |   |   |   |   | 1 |
| 2 | 3 | 4 | 5 | 6 | 7 | 8 |
| 9 | 10 | 11 | 12 | 13 | 14 | 15 |
| 16 | 17 | 18 | 19 | 20 | 21 | 22 |
| 23 | 24 | 25 | 26 | 27 | 28 | 29 |
| 30 | 31 |   |   |   |   |   |

### FEBRUARY

| S | M | T | W | T | F | S |
|---|---|---|---|---|---|---|
|   |   | 1 | 2 | 3 | 4 | 5 |
| 6 | 7 | 8 | 9 | 10 | 11 | 12 |
| 13 | 14 | 15 | 16 | 17 | 18 | 19 |
| 20 | 21 | 22 | 23 | 24 | 25 | 26 |
| 27 | 28 | 29 |   |   |   |   |

### MARCH

| S | M | T | W | T | F | S |
|---|---|---|---|---|---|---|
|   |   |   | 1 | 2 | 3 | 4 |
| 5 | 6 | 7 | 8 | 9 | 10 | 11 |
| 12 | 13 | 14 | 15 | 16 | 17 | 18 |
| 19 | 20 | 21 | 22 | 23 | 24 | 25 |
| 26 | 27 | 28 | 29 | 30 | 31 |   |

### APRIL

| S | M | T | W | T | F | S |
|---|---|---|---|---|---|---|
|   |   |   |   |   |   | 1 |
| 2 | 3 | 4 | 5 | 6 | 7 | 8 |
| 9 | 10 | 11 | 12 | 13 | 14 | 15 |
| 16 | 17 | 18 | 19 | 20 | 21 | 22 |
| 23 | 24 | 25 | 26 | 27 | 28 | 29 |
| 30 |   |   |   |   |   |   |

### MAY

| S | M | T | W | T | F | S |
|---|---|---|---|---|---|---|
|   | 1 | 2 | 3 | 4 | 5 | 6 |
| 7 | 8 | 9 | 10 | 11 | 12 | 13 |
| 14 | 15 | 16 | 17 | 18 | 19 | 20 |
| 21 | 22 | 23 | 24 | 25 | 26 | 27 |
| 28 | 29 | 30 | 31 |   |   |   |

### JUNE

| S | M | T | W | T | F | S |
|---|---|---|---|---|---|---|
|   |   |   |   | 1 | 2 | 3 |
| 4 | 5 | 6 | 7 | 8 | 9 | 10 |
| 11 | 12 | 13 | 14 | 15 | 16 | 17 |
| 18 | 19 | 20 | 21 | 22 | 23 | 24 |
| 25 | 26 | 27 | 28 | 29 | 30 |   |

# N

## JULY

| S | M | T | W | T | F | S |
|---|---|---|---|---|---|---|
|   |   |   |   |   |   | 1 |
| 2 | 3 | 4 | 5 | 6 | 7 | 8 |
| 9 | 10 | 11 | 12 | 13 | 14 | 15 |
| 16 | 17 | 18 | 19 | 20 | 21 | 22 |
| 23 | 24 | 25 | 26 | 27 | 28 | 29 |
| 30 | 31 |   |   |   |   |   |

## AUGUST

| S | M | T | W | T | F | S |
|---|---|---|---|---|---|---|
|   |   | 1 | 2 | 3 | 4 | 5 |
| 6 | 7 | 8 | 9 | 10 | 11 | 12 |
| 13 | 14 | 15 | 16 | 17 | 18 | 19 |
| 20 | 21 | 22 | 23 | 24 | 25 | 26 |
| 27 | 28 | 29 | 30 | 31 |   |   |

## SEPTEMBER

| S | M | T | W | T | F | S |
|---|---|---|---|---|---|---|
|   |   |   |   |   | 1 | 2 |
| 3 | 4 | 5 | 6 | 7 | 8 | 9 |
| 10 | 11 | 12 | 13 | 14 | 15 | 16 |
| 17 | 18 | 19 | 20 | 21 | 22 | 23 |
| 24 | 25 | 26 | 27 | 28 | 29 | 30 |

## OCTOBER

| S | M | T | W | T | F | S |
|---|---|---|---|---|---|---|
| 1 | 2 | 3 | 4 | 5 | 6 | 7 |
| 8 | 9 | 10 | 11 | 12 | 13 | 14 |
| 15 | 16 | 17 | 18 | 19 | 20 | 21 |
| 22 | 23 | 24 | 25 | 26 | 27 | 28 |
| 29 | 30 | 31 |   |   |   |   |

## NOVEMBER

| S | M | T | W | T | F | S |
|---|---|---|---|---|---|---|
|   |   |   | 1 | 2 | 3 | 4 |
| 5 | 6 | 7 | 8 | 9 | 10 | 11 |
| 12 | 13 | 14 | 15 | 16 | 17 | 18 |
| 19 | 20 | 21 | 22 | 23 | 24 | 25 |
| 26 | 27 | 28 | 29 | 30 |   |   |

## DECEMBER

| S | M | T | W | T | F | S |
|---|---|---|---|---|---|---|
|   |   |   |   |   | 1 | 2 |
| 3 | 4 | 5 | 6 | 7 | 8 | 9 |
| 10 | 11 | 12 | 13 | 14 | 15 | 16 |
| 17 | 18 | 19 | 20 | 21 | 22 | 23 |
| 24 | 25 | 26 | 27 | 28 | 29 | 30 |
| 31 |   |   |   |   |   |   |

# CHAPTER 5

# FINANCES AND CONVERSIONS

### Interest

Interest refers to the charge accrued for borrowing money or to payment made for loaning money. Interest is usually expressed in terms of percentage rates. There are two types of interest: simple interest and compound interest.

### *Simple interest*

Simple interest is calculated on the amount of money originally loaned, which is called the principal. The formula used to calculate simple interest is:

$$I = \frac{P \times R \times T}{100}$$

I = interest
P = principal
R = the percentage rate per unit time
T = the length of time over which the money is invested or loaned.

The final amount of money to which the principal will grow is called the sum, and is determined using the following formula:

$$S \text{ (sum)} = \frac{P(1 + R \times T)}{100}$$

## Compound interest

Unlike simple interest, which is paid only on the principal, compound interest is paid on the previous interest earned as well. Therefore, the sum increases at a much faster rate than with simple interest.

Compound interest is figured using the following formula:

$S = P (1 + i)n$

$i$ = the periodic interest

$n$ = the number of periods

## Simple interest

| Simple interest rates to add to $1000 percent per annum | | | | | |
|---|---|---|---|---|---|
| Period | 2.5% | 3% | 3.5% | 4% | 4.5% |
| 1 day | 0.068 | 0.082 | 0.096 | 0.110 | 0.123 |
| 2 days | 0.137 | 0.164 | 0.192 | 0.219 | 0.247 |
| 3 days | 0.205 | 0.247 | 0.288 | 0.329 | 0.370 |
| 4 days | 0.274 | 0.329 | 0.384 | 0.438 | 0.493 |
| 5 days | 0.342 | 0.411 | 0.479 | 0.548 | 0.616 |
| 6 days | 0.411 | 0.493 | 0.575 | 0.658 | 0.740 |
| 30 days | 2.055 | 2.466 | 2.877 | 3.288 | 3.699 |
| 60 days | 4.110 | 4.932 | 5.753 | 6.575 | 7.397 |
| 1090 days | 6.164 | 7.397 | 8.630 | 9.863 | 11.096 |
| 180 days | 12.329 | 14.795 | 17.260 | 19.726 | 22.192 |
| 360 days | 24.658 | 29.589 | 34.521 | 39.452 | 44.384 |
| 1 year | 25.000 | 30.000 | 35.000 | 40.000 | 45.000 |

| Simple interest added on to a principal of $100 percent per annum | | | | | |
|---|---|---|---|---|---|
| Period | 7% | 8% | 9% | 10% | 11% |
| 1 year | 107.00 | 108.00 | 109.00 | 110.00 | 111.00 |
| 5 years | 135.00 | 140.00 | 145.00 | 150.00 | 155.00 |
| 10 years | 170.00 | 180.00 | 190.00 | 200.00 | 210.00 |
| 20 years | 240.00 | 260.00 | 280.00 | 300.00 | 320.00 |
| 30 years | 310.00 | 340.00 | 370.00 | 400.00 | 430.00 |
| 40 years | 380.00 | 420.00 | 460.00 | 500.00 | 540.00 |
| 50 years | 450.00 | 500.00 | 550.00 | 600.00 | 650.00 |

## Simple interest rates to add to $1000
### percent per annum

| 5% | 5.5% | 6% | 6.5% | 7% |
|---|---|---|---|---|
| 0.137 | 0.151 | 0.164 | 0.178 | 0.192 |
| 0.274 | 0.301 | 0.389 | 0.356 | 0.384 |
| 0.411 | 0.452 | 0.493 | 0.534 | 0.575 |
| 0.548 | 0.603 | 0.658 | 0.712 | 0.767 |
| 0.685 | 0.753 | 0.822 | 0.890 | 0.959 |
| 0.822 | 0.904 | 0.986 | 1.068 | 1.151 |
| 4.110 | 4.521 | 4.932 | 5.342 | 5.753 |
| 8.219 | 9.041 | 9.863 | 10.685 | 11.507 |
| 12.329 | 13.562 | 14.795 | 16.027 | 17.260 |
| 24.658 | 27.123 | 29.589 | 32.055 | 34.521 |
| 49.315 | 54.247 | 59.178 | 64.110 | 69.041 |
| 50.000 | 55.000 | 60.000 | 65.000 | 70.000 |

## Simple interest added on to a principal of $100
### percent per annum

| 12% | 13% | 14% | 15% |
|---|---|---|---|
| 112.00 | 113.00 | 114.00 | 115.00 |
| 160.00 | 165.00 | 170.00 | 175.00 |
| 220.00 | 230.00 | 240.00 | 250.00 |
| 340.00 | 360.00 | 380.00 | 400.00 |
| 460.00 | 490.00 | 520.00 | 550.00 |
| 580.00 | 620.00 | 660.00 | 700.00 |
| 700.00 | 750.00 | 800.00 | 850.00 |

## Compound interest

The table below shows the compound interest paid on a principal of $100. The interest rate is in percent per annum.

| Period | 4% | 5% | 6% | 7% | 8% |
|--------|------|------|------|------|------|
| 1 day | 0.011 | 0.014 | 0.016 | 0.019 | 0.02 |
| 1 week | 0.077 | 0.096 | 0.115 | 0.135 | 0.15 |
| 6 months | 2.00 | 2.50 | 3.00 | 3.50 | 4.00 |
| 1 year | 4.00 | 5.00 | 6.00 | 7.00 | 8.00 |
| 2 years | 8.16 | 10.25 | 12.36 | 14.49 | 16.64 |
| 3 years | 12.49 | 15.76 | 19.10 | 22.50 | 25.97 |
| 4 years | 16.99 | 21.55 | 26.25 | 31.08 | 36.05 |
| 5 years | 21.67 | 27.63 | 33.82 | 40.26 | 46.93 |
| 6 years | 26.53 | 34.01 | 41.85 | 50.07 | 58.69 |
| 7 years | 31.59 | 40.71 | 50.36 | 60.58 | 71.38 |
| 8 years | 36.86 | 47.75 | 59.38 | 71.82 | 85.09 |
| 9 years | 42.33 | 55.13 | 68.95 | 83.85 | 99.90 |
| 10 years | 48.02 | 62.89 | 79.08 | 96.72 | 115.89 |

## Comparing the two

As you can see, money grows much more quickly with compound interest than with simple interest. For example, compare below the amount of time required for any amount of money to double itself with simple interest and with compound interest:

| 9% | 10% | 12% | 14% | 16% |
|---|---|---|---|---|
| 0.025 | 0.027 | 0.033 | 0.038 | 0.044 |
| 0.173 | 0.192 | 0.231 | 0.269 | 0.308 |
| 4.50 | 5.00 | 6.00 | 7.00 | 8.00 |
| 9.00 | 10.00 | 12.00 | 14.00 | 16.00 |
| 18.81 | 21.00 | 25.44 | 29.96 | 34.56 |
| 29.50 | 33.10 | 40.49 | 48.15 | 56.09 |
| 41.16 | 46.41 | 57.35 | 68.90 | 81.06 |
| 53.86 | 61.05 | 76.23 | 92.54 | 110.03 |
| 67.71 | 77.16 | 97.38 | 119.50 | 143.64 |
| 82.80 | 94.87 | 121.07 | 150.23 | 182.62 |
| 99.26 | 114.36 | 147.60 | 185.26 | 227.84 |
| 17.19 | 135.79 | 177.31 | 225.19 | 280.30 |
| 36.74 | 150.37 | 210.50 | 270.72 | 341.14 |

| Rate | Simple | Compound |
|---|---|---|
| 7% | 14 yrs, 104 days | 10 yrs, 89 days |
| 10% | 10 yrs | 7 yrs, 100 days |

## The Mortgage Calculator

One of the most important purchases you will ever make will be buying a home. The following chart demonstrates the various interest rates banks and other lending institutions are charging for sums close to average housing costs:

| 5.875% | 6.000% | 6.125% | 6.250% | 6.375% | 6.500% | Mortg. Amt |
|--------|--------|--------|--------|--------|--------|------------|
| 473.23 | 479.64 | 486.09 | 492.57 | 499.10 | 505.65 | 80,000.0 |
| 502.81 | 509.62 | 516.47 | 523.36 | 530.29 | 537.26 | 85,000.0 |
| 532.38 | 539.60 | 546.85 | 554.15 | 561.48 | 568.86 | 90,000.0 |
| 561.96 | 569.57 | 577.23 | 584.93 | 592.68 | 600.46 | 95,000.0 |
| 591.54 | 599.55 | 607.61 | 615.72 | 623.87 | 632.07 | 100,000.0 |
| **5.875%** | **6.000%** | **6.125%** | **6.250%** | **6.375%** | **6.500%** | **Mortg. Amt** |
| 606.33 | 614.54 | 622.80 | 631.11 | 639.47 | 647.87 | 102,500.0 |
| 621.11 | 629.53 | 637.99 | 646.50 | 655.06 | 663.67 | 105,000.0 |
| 635.90 | 644.52 | 653.18 | 661.90 | 670.66 | 679.47 | 107,500.0 |
| 650.69 | 659.51 | 668.37 | 677.29 | 686.26 | 695.27 | 110,000.0 |
| 665.48 | 674.49 | 683.56 | 692.68 | 701.85 | 711.08 | 112,500.0 |
| **5.875%** | **6.000%** | **6.125%** | **6.250%** | **6.375%** | **6.500%** | **Mortg. Amt** |
| 680.27 | 689.48 | 698.75 | 708.07 | 717.45 | 726.88 | 115,000.0 |
| 695.06 | 704.47 | 713.94 | 723.47 | 733.05 | 742.68 | 117,500.0 |
| 709.85 | 719.46 | 729.13 | 738.86 | 748.64 | 758.48 | 120,000.0 |
| 724.63 | 734.45 | 744.32 | 754.25 | 764.24 | 774.28 | 122,500.0 |
| 739.42 | 749.44 | 759.51 | 769.65 | 779.84 | 790.09 | 125,000.0 |

| 6.625% | 6.750% | 6.875% | 7.000% | 7.125% | 7.250% |
|--------|--------|--------|--------|--------|--------|
| 512.25 | 518.88 | 525.54 | 532.24 | 538.97 | 545.74 |
| 544.26 | 551.31 | 558.39 | 565.51 | 572.66 | 579.85 |
| 576.28 | 583.74 | 591.24 | 598.77 | 606.35 | 613.96 |
| 608.30 | 616.17 | 624.08 | 632.04 | 640.03 | 648.07 |
| 640.31 | 648.60 | 656.93 | 665.30 | 673.72 | 682.18 |
| 6.625% | 6.750% | 6.875% | 7.000% | 7.125% | 7.250% |
| 656.32 | 664.81 | 673.35 | 681.94 | 690.56 | 699.23 |
| 672.33 | 681.03 | 689.78 | 698.57 | 707.40 | 716.29 |
| 688.33 | 697.24 | 706.20 | 715.20 | 724.25 | 733.34 |
| 704.34 | 713.46 | 722.62 | 731.83 | 741.09 | 750.39 |
| 720.35 | 729.67 | 739.04 | 748.47 | 757.93 | 767.45 |
| 6.625% | 6.750% | 6.875% | 7.000% | 7.125% | 7.250% |
| 736.36 | 745.89 | 755.47 | 765.10 | 774.78 | 784.50 |
| 752.37 | 762.10 | 771.89 | 781.73 | 791.62 | 801.56 |
| 768.37 | 778.32 | 788.31 | 798.36 | 808.46 | 818.61 |
| 784.38 | 794.53 | 804.74 | 815.00 | 825.31 | 835.67 |
| 800.39 | 810.75 | 821.16 | 831.63 | 842.15 | 852.72 |

| 5.875% | 6.000% | 6.125% | 6.250% | 6.375% | 6.500% | Mortg. Ar |
|---|---|---|---|---|---|---|
| 754.21 | 764.43 | 774.70 | 785.04 | 795.43 | 805.89 | 127,500 |
| 769.00 | 779.42 | 789.89 | 800.43 | 811.03 | 821.69 | 130,000 |
| 783.79 | 794.40 | 805.08 | 815.83 | 826.63 | 837.49 | 132,500 |
| 798.58 | 809.39 | 820.27 | 831.22 | 842.22 | 853.29 | 135,00 0 |
| 813.36 | 824.38 | 835.46 | 846.61 | 857.82 | 869.09 | 137,500 |
| 5.875% | 6.000% | 6.125% | 6.250% | 6.375% | 6.500% | Mortg. Ar |
| 828.15 | 839.37 | 850.65 | 862.00 | 873.42 | 884.90 | 140,000 |
| 842.94 | 854.36 | 865.85 | 877.40 | 889.01 | 900.70 | 142,500 |
| 857.73 | 869.35 | 881.04 | 892.79 | 904.61 | 916.50 | 145,000 |
| 872.52 | 884.34 | 896.23 | 908.18 | 920.21 | 932.30 | 147,500 |
| 887.31 | 899.33 | 911.42 | 923.58 | 935.80 | 948.10 | 150,000 |
| 5.875% | 6.000% | 6.125% | 6.250% | 6.375% | 6.500% | Mortg. Ar |
| 902.10 | 914.31 | 926.61 | 938.97 | 951.40 | 963.90 | 152,500 |
| 916.88 | 929.30 | 941.80 | 954.36 | 967.00 | 979.71 | 155,000 |
| 931.67 | 944.29 | 956.99 | 969.75 | 982.60 | 995.51 | 157,500 |
| 946.46 | 959.28 | 972.18 | 985.15 | 998.19 | 1,011.31 | 160,000 |
| 961.25 | 974.27 | 987.37 | 1,000.54 | 1,013.79 | 1,027.11 | 162,500 |
| 5.875% | 6.000% | 6.125% | 6.250% | 6.375% | 6.500% | Mortg. Ar |
| 976.04 | 989.26 | 1,002.56 | 1,015.93 | 1,029.39 | 1,042.91 | 165,000 |
| 990.83 | 1,004.25 | 1,017.75 | 1,031.33 | 1,044.98 | 1,058.71 | 167,500 |
| 1,005.61 | 1,019.24 | 1,032.94 | 1,046.72 | 1,060.58 | 1,074.52 | 170,000 |
| 1,020.40 | 1,034.22 | 1,048.13 | 1,062.11 | 1,076.18 | 1,090.32 | 172,500 |
| 1,035.19 | 1,049.21 | 1,063.32 | 1,077.51 | 1,091.77 | 1,106.12 | 175,000 |

| 6.625% | 6.750% | 6.875% | 7.000% | 7.125% | 7.250% |
|---|---|---|---|---|---|
| 816.40 | 826.96 | 837.58 | 848.26 | 858.99 | 869.77 |
| 832.40 | 843.18 | 854.01 | 864.89 | 875.83 | 886.83 |
| 848.41 | 859.39 | 870.43 | 881.53 | 892.68 | 903.88 |
| 864.42 | 875.61 | 886.85 | 898.16 | 909.52 | 920.94 |
| 880.43 | 891.82 | 903.28 | 914.79 | 926.36 | 937.99 |
| 6.625% | 6.750% | 6.875% | 7.000% | 7.125% | 7.250% |
| 896.44 | 908.04 | 919.70 | 931.42 | 943.21 | 955.05 |
| 912.44 | 924.25 | 936.12 | 948.06 | 960.05 | 972.10 |
| 928.45 | 940.47 | 952.55 | 964.69 | 976.89 | 989.16 |
| 944.46 | 956.68 | 968.97 | 981.32 | 993.73 | 1,006.21 |
| 960.47 | 972.90 | 985.39 | 997.95 | 1,010.58 | 1,023.26 |
| 6.625% | 6.750% | 6.875% | 7.000% | 7.125% | 7.250% |
| 976.47 | 989.11 | 1,001.82 | 1,014.59 | 1,027.42 | 1,040.32 |
| 992.48 | 1,005.33 | 1,018.24 | 1,031.22 | 1,044.26 | 1,057.37 |
| ,008.49 | 1,021.54 | 1,034.66 | 1,047.85 | 1,061.11 | 1,074.43 |
| ,024.50 | 1,037.76 | 1,051.09 | 1,064.48 | 1,077.95 | 1,091.48 |
| ,040.51 | 1,053.97 | 1,067.51 | 1,001.12 | 1,004.79 | 1,108.54 |
| 6.625% | 6.750% | 6.875% | 7.000% | 7.125% | 7.250% |
| ,056.51 | 1,070.19 | 1,083.93 | 1,097.75 | 1,111.64 | 1,125.59 |
| ,072.52 | 1,086.40 | 1,100.36 | 1,114.38 | 1,128.48 | 1,142.65 |
| ,088.53 | 1,102.62 | 1,116.78 | 1,131.01 | 1,145.32 | 1,159.70 |
| ,104.54 | 1,118.83 | 1,133.20 | 1,147.65 | 1,162.16 | 1,176.75 |
| ,120.54 | 1,135.05 | 1,149.63 | 1,164.28 | 1,179.01 | 1,193.81 |

| 5.875% | 6.000% | 6.125% | 6.250% | 6.375% | 6.500% | Mortg. A |
|---|---|---|---|---|---|---|
| 1,049.98 | 1,064.20 | 1,078.51 | 1,092.90 | 1,107.37 | 1,121.92 | 177,500 |
| 1,064.77 | 1,079.19 | 1,093.70 | 1,108.29 | 1,122.97 | 1,137.72 | 180,000 |
| 1,079.56 | 1,094.18 | 1,108.89 | 1,123.68 | 1,138.56 | 1,153.52 | 182,500 |
| 1,094.34 | 1,109.17 | 1,124.08 | 1,139.08 | 1,154.16 | 1,169.33 | 185,000 |
| 1,109.13 | 1,124.16 | 1,139.27 | 1,154.47 | 1,169.76 | 1,185.13 | 187,500 |
| 5.875% | 6.000% | 6.125% | 6.250% | 6.375% | 6.500% | Mortg. A |
| 1,123.92 | 1,139.15 | 1,154.46 | 1,169.86 | 1,185.35 | 1,200.93 | 190,000 |
| 1,138.71 | 1,154.13 | 1,169.65 | 1,185.26 | 1,200.95 | 1,216.73 | 192,500 |
| 1,153.50 | 1,169.12 | 1,184.84 | 1,200.65 | 1,216.55 | 1,232.53 | 195,000 |
| 1,168.29 | 1,184.11 | 1,200.03 | 1,216.04 | 1,232.14 | 1,248.33 | 197,500 |
| 1,183.08 | 1,199.10 | 1,215.22 | 1,231.43 | 1,247.74 | 1,264.14 | 200,000 |
| 5.875% | 6.000% | 6.125% | 6.250% | 6.375% | 6.500% | Mortg. A |
| 1,197.86 | 1,214.09 | 1,230.41 | 1,246.83 | 1,263.34 | 1,279.94 | 202,500 |
| 1,212.65 | 1,229.08 | 1,245.60 | 1,262.22 | 1,278.93 | 1,295.74 | 205,000 |
| 1,227.44 | 1,244.07 | 1,260.79 | 1,277.61 | 1,294.53 | 1,311.54 | 207,500 |
| 1,242.23 | 1,259.06 | 1,275.98 | 1,293.01 | 1,310.13 | 1,327.34 | 210,000 |

| 6.625% | 6.750% | 6.875% | 7.000% | 7.125% | 7.250% |
|---|---|---|---|---|---|
| 1,136.55 | 1,151.26 | 1,166.05 | 1,180.91 | 1,195.85 | 1,210.86 |
| 1,152.56 | 1,167.48 | 1,182.47 | 1,197.54 | 1,212.69 | 1,227.92 |
| 1,168.57 | 1,183.69 | 1,198.90 | 1,214.18 | 1,229.54 | 1,244.97 |
| 1,184.58 | 1,199.91 | 1,215.32 | 1,230.81 | 1,246.38 | 1,262.03 |
| 1,200.58 | 1,216.12 | 1,231.74 | 1,247.44 | 1,263.22 | 1,279.08 |
| **6.625%** | **6.750%** | **6.875%** | **7.000%** | **7.125%** | **7.250%** |
| 1,216.59 | 1,232.34 | 1,248.16 | 1,264.07 | 1,280.07 | 1,296.13 |
| 1,232.60 | 1,248.55 | 1,264.59 | 1,280.71 | 1,296.91 | 1,313.19 |
| 1,248.61 | 1,264.77 | 1,281.01 | 1,297.34 | 1,313.75 | 1,330.24 |
| 1,264.61 | 1,280.98 | 1,297.43 | 1,313.97 | 1,330.59 | 1,347.30 |
| 1,280.62 | 1,297.20 | 1,313.86 | 1,330.60 | 1,347.44 | 1,364.35 |
| **6.625%** | **6.750%** | **6.875%** | **7.000%** | **7.125%** | **7.250%** |
| 1,296.63 | 1,313.41 | 1,330.28 | 1,347.24 | 1,364.28 | 1,381.41 |
| 1,312.64 | 1,329.63 | 1,346.70 | 1,363.87 | 1,381.12 | 1,398.46 |
| 1,328.65 | 1,345.84 | 1,363.13 | 1,380.50 | 1,397.97 | 1,415.52 |
| 1,344.65 | 1,362.06 | 1,379.55 | 1,397.14 | 1,414.01 | 1,432.57 |

## The Tip Calculator

The word "tip" is actually an acronym for the phrase "to insure promptness." What was once an additional payment based on good service has become a standardized transaction for a variety of different services. But when do you tip, and how much do you give? The following chart lists standard bills with standard tips: give 15% for "as expected" service; 20% if your service was found to be exceptional.

| Bill | 15% tip | 20% tip |
|------|---------|---------|
| 5 | $ 0.75 | $ 1.00 |
| 10 | $ 1.50 | $ 2.00 |
| 15 | $ 2.25 | $ 3.00 |
| 20 | $ 3.00 | $ 4.00 |
| 25 | $ 3.75 | $ 5.00 |
| 30 | $ 4.50 | $ 6.00 |
| 35 | $ 5.25 | $ 7.00 |
| 40 | $ 6.00 | $ 8.00 |
| 45 | $ 6.75 | $ 9.00 |
| 50 | $ 7.50 | $ 10.00 |
| 55 | $ 8.25 | $ 11.00 |
| 60 | $ 9.00 | $ 12.00 |
| 65 | $ 9.75 | $ 13.00 |
| 70 | $ 10.50 | $ 14.00 |
| 75 | $ 11.25 | $ 15.00 |
| 80 | $ 12.00 | $ 16.00 |
| 85 | $ 12.75 | $ 17.00 |

| Bill | 15% tip | 20% tip |
|------|---------|---------|
| 90 | $ 13.50 | $ 18.00 |
| 95 | $ 14.25 | $ 19.00 |
| 100 | $ 15.00 | $ 20.00 |
| 105 | $ 15.75 | $ 21.00 |
| 110 | $ 16.50 | $ 22.00 |
| 115 | $ 17.25 | $ 23.00 |
| 120 | $ 18.00 | $ 24.00 |
| 125 | $ 18.75 | $ 25.00 |
| 130 | $ 19.50 | $ 26.00 |
| 135 | $ 20.25 | $ 27.00 |
| 140 | $ 21.00 | $ 28.00 |
| 145 | $ 21.75 | $ 29.00 |
| 150 | $ 22.50 | $ 30.00 |
| 155 | $ 23.25 | $ 31.00 |
| 160 | $ 24.00 | $ 32.00 |
| 165 | $ 24.75 | $ 33.00 |
| 170 | $ 25.50 | $ 34.00 |
| 175 | $ 26.25 | $ 35.00 |
| 180 | $ 27.00 | $ 36.00 |
| 185 | $ 27.75 | $ 37.00 |
| 190 | $ 28.50 | $ 38.00 |
| 195 | $ 29.25 | $ 39.00 |
| 200 | $ 30.00 | $ 40.00 |

### International Gratuities

Throughout the world, tips have become an important part of the hotel and restaurant industry. In some places, everyone from the waiter to porters to proprietors depend on gratuities as part of their wages. Here's a quick reference for the sophisticated traveler:

## RESTAURANT TIPS BY COUNTRY

| Country | Tip |
| --- | --- |
| United States | 15%-20% |
| France | 12%-15% |
| U.K. | 10%-12% |
| Japan | 10%-20% |
| Germany | 10%-15% |
| Hong Kong | 10%-15% |
| Italy | 10% |
| Mexico | 10% |

| Comment |
| --- |
| Expected, but usually not included in bill. |
| Usually included in restaurant bills. |
| Usually included in restaurant bill. |
| Usually included in restaurant bill; otherwise, tipping not common. |
| Service charge usually included in restaurant bill; small additional tip is generally considered appropriate. |
| Tipping common, but not included. |
| Tips expected, but not included. |
| Tipping common, but not included. |

## International Currency Table

The following table lists all of the world's currencies.

| Currency Name | Country | Major Unit |
|---|---|---|
| Andorran Franc | Andorra | franc |
| Andorran Peseta | Andorra | peseta |
| | United Arab Emirates | dirham |
| Afghanistan Afghani | Afghanistan | afghani |
| Albanian Lek | Albania | Lek |
| NL Antillian Guilder | Netherlands Antilles | N.A. guilder |
| | Angola | new kwanza (kwanza reajustado) |
| Argentine Peso | Argentina | nuevo peso |
| Austrian Schilling | Austria | schilling |
| Australian Dollar | Australia | dollar |
| Aruban Florin | Aruba | florin |
| Barbados Dollar | Barbados | dollar |
| Bangladeshi Taka | Bangladesh | taka |
| Belgian Franc | Belgium | franc |
| Bulgarian Lev | Bulgaria | lev |
| Bahraini Dinar | Bahrain | dinar |
| Burundi Franc | Burundi | franc |
| Bermudian Dollar | Bermuda | dollar |
| Brunei Dollar | Brunei Darussalam | dollar (a.k.a. ringitt) |
| Bolivian Boliviano | Bolivia | boliviano |

...riginal currencies replaced by the euro are still listed.

| Minor Unit | Equivalence |
|---|---|
| centime | 100 centime = franc |
| centimos | 100 centimos = peseta |
| fils | 100 fils = dirham |
|  | 100 fils = dirham |
| puls | 100 puls = afghani |
| qindarka | 100 qindarka = Lek |
| cents | 100 cents = N.A. guilder |
| lwei | 100 lwei = new kwanza (kwanza reajustado) |
| centavos | 100 centavos = nuevo peso |
| groschen | 100 groschen = schilling |
| cents | 100 cents = dollar |
| cent | 100 cent = florin |
| cents | 100 cents = dollar |
| paisa | 100 paisa = taka |
| centimes | 100 centimes = franc |
| stotinki | 100 stotinki = lev |
| fils | 1000 fils = dinar |
| centimes | 100 centimes = franc |
| cents | 100 cents = dollar |
| cents | 100 cents = dollar (a.k.a. ringitt) |
| centavos | 100 centavos = boliviano |

| Currency Name | Country | Major Unit |
|---|---|---|
| Brazilian Real | Brazil | real |
| Bahamian Dollar | Bahamas | dollar |
| Bhutan Ngultrum | Bhutan | ngultrum |
| Botswana Pula | Botswana | pula |
| Belize Dollar | Belize | dollar |
| Canadian Dollar | Canada | dollar |
| Swiss Franc | Liechtenstein | franc |
| Swiss Franc | Switzerland | franc |
| Chilean Peso | Chile | new peso |
| Chinese Yuan Renminbi | China | yuan renminb |
| Colombian Peso | Colombia | peso |
| Costa Rican Colon | Costa Rica | colon |
| Cuban Peso | Cuba | peso |
| | Cape Verde | escudo |
| Cyprus Pound | Cyprus | pound |
| Czech Koruna | Czech Republic | koruna |
| German Mark | Germany | deutsche mark |
| Djibouti Franc | Djibouti | franc |
| Danish Krone | Denmark, Greenland, Faroe Islands | krone |
| Dominican Peso | Dominican Republic | peso |
| Algerian Dinar | Algeria | dinar |
| Ecuador Sucre | Ecuador | sucre |
| Estonian Kroon | Estonia | kroon |

| Minor Unit | Equivalence |
|---|---|
| centavos | 100 centavos = real |
| cents | 100 cents = dollar |
| chetrum | 100 chetrum = ngultrum |
| thebe | 100 thebe = pula |
| cents | 100 cents = dollar |
| cents | 100 cents = dollar |
| centimes | 100 centimes = franc |
| centimes | 100 centimes = franc |
| centavos | 100 centavos = new peso |
| jiao | 10 jiao = yuan renminbi |
| centavos | 100 centavos = peso |
| centimos | 100 centimos = colon |
| centavos | 100 centavos = peso |
| centavos | 100 centavos = escudo |
| cents | 100 cents = pound |
| haliers | 100 haliers = koruna |
| pfennige | 100 pfennige = deutsche mark |
| centimes | 100 centimes = franc |
| ˆre | 100 ˆre = krone |
| centavos | 100 centavos = peso |
| centimes | 100 centimes = dinar |
| centavos | 100 centavos = sucre |
| senti | 100 senti = kroon |

| Currency Name | Country | Major Unit |
|---|---|---|
| Egyptian Pound | Egypt | pound |
| Spanish Peseta | Spain | peseta |
| Spanish Peseta | Western Sahara | peseta |
| Ethiopian Birr | Ethiopia | birr |
| Euro | Austria, Belgium, Finland, France, Germany, Ireland, Italy, Luxembourg, Netherlands, Portugal, Spain | euro |
| Finnish Markka | Finland | markka a.k.a. finmark) |
| Fiji Dollar | Fiji | dollar |
| | Falkland Islands | pound |
| French Franc | France, French Guiana, Guadeloupe, Martinique, Mayotte, Monaco, Reunion, Saint Pierre & Miquelon | franc |
| | British Indian Ocean Territory, South Georgia and The South Sandwich Islands, United Kingdom, British Virgin Islands | pound |
| Ghanaian Cedi | Ghana | new cedi |

| Minor Unit | Equivalence |
|---|---|
| milliemes, piasters | 1000 milliemes = pound, 100 piasters = pound |
| centimos | 100 centimos = peseta |
| centimos | 100 centimos = peseta |
| cents | 100 cents = birr |
| euro-cents | 100 euro-cents = euro |
| pennia | 100 pennia = markka a.k.a. finmark) |
| cents | 100 cents = dollar |
| pence | 100 pence = pound |
| centimes | 100 centimes = franc |
| pence | 100 pence = pound |
| pesewas | 100 pesewas = new cedi |

| Currency Name | Country | Major Unit |
|---|---|---|
| Gibraltar Pound | Gibraltar | pound |
| Gambian Dalasi | Gambia | dalasi |
| Guinea Franc | Guinea | franc |
| Greek Drachma | Greece | drachma |
| Guatemalen Quetzal | Guatemala | quetzal |
| Guyanan Dollar | Guyana | dollar |
| Hong Kong Dollar | Hong Kong | dollar |
| Honduran Lempira | Honduras | lempira |
| Croatian Kuna | Croatia | kuna |
| Haitian Gourde | Haiti | gourde |
| Hungarian Forint | Hungary | forint |
| Indonesian Rupiah | East Timor | rupiah |
| Indonesian Rupiah | Indonesia | rupiah |
| Irish Punt | Ireland | punt or pound |
| Israeli New Shekel | Israel | new shekel |
| Indian Rupee | India | rupee |
| Iraqi Dinar | Iraq | dinar |
| Iranian Rial | Iran, Islamic Republic of | toman |
| Iceland Krona | Iceland | krûna |
| Italian Lira | Italy, San Marino, Holy See (Vatican City State) | lira |
| Jamaican Dollar | Jamaica | dollar |
| Jordanian Dinar | Jordan | dinar |
| Japanese Yen | Japan | yen |
| Kenyan Shilling | Kenya | shilling |

| Minor Unit | Equivalence |
|---|---|
| pence | 100 pence = pound |
| butut | 100 butut = dalasi |
| centimes | 100 centimes = franc |
| lepta | 100 lepta = drachma |
| centavos | 100 centavos = quetzal |
| cents | 100 cents = dollar |
| cents | 100 cents = dollar |
| centavos | 100 centavos = lempira |
| lipas | 100 lipas = kuna |
| centimes | 100 centimes = gourde |
| fillér | 100 fillér = forint |
| sen | 100 sen = rupiah |
| sen | 100 sen = rupiah |
| pingin | 100 pingin = punt or pound |
| new agorot | 100 new agorot = new shekel |
| paise | 100 paise = rupee |
| fils | 1000 fils = dinar |
| rial | 10 rial = toman |
| aurar | 100 aurar = krûna |
| centesimi | 100 centesimi = lira |
| cents | 100 cents = dollar |
| fils | 1000 fils = dinar |
| sen | 100 sen = yen |
| cents | 100 cents = shilling |

| Currency Name | Country | Major Unit |
|---|---|---|
| Kampuchean Riel | Cambodia | new riel |
| Comoros Franc | Comoros | franc |
| North Korean Won | Korea, Democratic People's Republic of | won |
| Korean Won | Korea, Republic of | won |
| Kuwaiti Dinar | Kuwait | dinar |
| | Cayman Islands | dollar |
| Kazakhstan Tenge | Kazakstan | tenge |
| Lao Kip | Lao People's Democratic Republic | new kip |
| Lebanese Pound | Lebanon | pound (livre) |
| Sri Lanka Rupee | Sri Lanka | rupee |
| Liberian Dollar | Liberia | dollar |
| Lesotho Loti | Lesotho | loti, pl., malot |
| Lithuanian Litas | Lithuania | litas, pl., litai |
| Luxembourg Franc | Luxembourg | franc |
| Latvian Lats | Latvia | lat |
| Libyan Dinar | Libyan Arab Jamahiriya | dinar |
| Moroccan Dirham | Morocco | dirham |
| Malagasy Franc | Madagascar | ariary |
| Myanmar Kyat | Myanmar | kyat |
| Mongolian Tugrik | Mongolia | tugrik |
| Macau Pataca | Macau | pataca |
| | Mauritania | ouguiya |
| Maltese Lira | Malta | lira, pl., liri |

| Minor Unit | Equivalence |
| --- | --- |
| sen | 100 sen = new riel |
| centimes | 100 centimes = franc |
| chon | 100 chon = won |
| | |
| chon | 100 chon = won |
| fils | 1000 fils = dinar |
| cents | 100 cents = dollar |
| tiyn | 100 tiyn = tenge |
| at | 100 at = new kip |
| | |
| piastres | 100 piastres = pound (livre) |
| cents | 100 cents = rupee |
| cents | 100 cents = dollar |
| lisente | 100 lisente = loti, pl., maloti |
| centu | 100 centu = litas, pl., litai |
| centimes | 100 centimes = franc |
| santims | 100 santims = lat |
| dirhams | 1000 dirhams = dinar |
| | |
| centimes | 100 centimes = dirham |
| centimes, francs | 100 centimes = francs, 5 francs = ariary |
| pyas | 100 pyas = kyat |
| mongos | 100 mongos = tugrik |
| avos | 100 avos = pataca |
| khoums | 5 khoums = ouguiya |
| cents | 100 cents = lira, pl., liri |

| Currency Name | Country | Major Unit |
|---|---|---|
| Mauritius Rupee | Mauritius | rupee |
| Maldive Rufiyaa | Maldives | rufiyaa |
| Malawi Kwacha | Malawi | kwacha |
| Mexican Peso | Mexico | peso |
| Malaysian Ringgit | Malaysia | ringgit |
| | Mozambique | metical |
| Namibia Dollar | Namibia | dollar |
| Nigerian Naira | Nigeria | naira |
| | Nicaragua | gold cordoba |
| Dutch Guilder | Netherlands | guilder (a.k.a. |
| Norwegian Kroner | Norway, Bouvet Island, Svalbard and Jan Mayen | krone |
| Nepalese Rupee | Nepal | rupee |
| New Zealand Dollar | New Zealand, Cook Islands, Niue, Pitcairn, Tokelau | dollar |
| Omani Rial | Oman | rial |
| | Panama | balboa |
| | Peru | new sol |
| | Papua New Guinea | kina |
| Philippine Peso | Philippines | peso |
| Pakistan Rupee | Pakistan | rupee |
| Polish Zloty | Poland | zloty |
| | Portugal | escudo |
| Paraguay Guarani | Paraguay | guarani |
| Qatari Rial | Qatar | riyal |

| Minor Unit | Equivalence |
|---|---|
| cents | 100 cents = rupee |
| lari | 100 lari = rufiyaa |
| tambala | 100 tambala = kwacha |
| centavo | 100 centavo = peso |
| sen | 100 sen = ringgit |
| centavos | 100 centavos = metical |
| cents | 100 cents = dollar |
| kobo | 100 kobo = naira |
| centavos | 100 centavos = gold cordoba |
| cents | 100 cents = guilder (a.k.a. florin) |
| ˆre | 100 ˆre = krone |
| | |
| paise | 100 paise = rupee |
| cents | 100 cents = dollar |
| | |
| baizas | 1000 baizas = rial |
| centesimos | 100 centesimos = balboa |
| centimos | 100 centimos = new sol |
| toeas | 100 toeas = kina |
| centavos | 100 centavos = peso |
| paisa | 100 paisa = rupee |
| groszy | 100 groszy = zloty |
| centavos | 100 centavos = escudo |
| centimos | 100 centimos = guarani |
| dirhams | 100 dirhams = riyal |

| Currency Name | Country | Major Unit |
|---|---|---|
| Romanian Leu | Romania | leu |
| Russian Rouble | Russian Federation | rouble |
| Russian Rouble | Tajikistan | rouble |
| Saudi Riyal | Saudi Arabia | riyal |
| | Solomon Islands | dollar |
| Seychelles Rupee | Seychelles | rupee |
| Sudanese Dinar | Sudan | dinar |
| Sudanese Pound | Sudan | pound |
| Swedish Krona | Sweden | krona |
| Singapore Dollar | Singapore | dollar |
| St. Helena Pound | Saint Helena | pound |
| Slovenian Tolar | Slovenia | tolar |
| Slovak Koruna | Slovakia | koruna |
| Sierra Leone Leone | Sierra Leone | leone |
| Somali Shilling | Somalia | shilling |
| Suriname Guilder | Suriname | guilder |
| | Sao Tome and Principe | dobra |
| El Salvador Colon | El Salvador | colon |
| Syrian Pound | Syrian Arab Republic | pound |
| Swaziland Lilangeni | Swaziland | lilangeni, pl., emalangeni |
| Thai Baht | Thailand | baht |
| Tunisian Dinar | Tunisia | dinar |
| Tongan Pa'anga | Tonga | pa'anga |
| Turkish Lira | Turkey | lira |

| Minor Unit | Equivalence |
| --- | --- |
| bani | 100 bani = leu |
| kopecks | 100 kopecks = rouble |
| kopecks | 100 kopecks = rouble |
| halalas | 100 halalas = riyal |
| cents | 100 cents = dollar |
| cents | 100 cents = rupee |
| piastres | 100 piastres = dinar |
| piastres | 100 piastres = pound |
| ˆre | 100 ˆre = krona |
| cents | 100 cents = dollar |
| new | 100 new = pound |
| stotinov | 100 stotinov = tolar |
| haliers | 100 haliers = koruna |
| cents | 100 cents = leone |
| centesimi | 100 centesimi = shilling |
| cents | 100 cents = guilder |
| centimos | 100 centimos = dobra |
| centavos | 100 centavos = colon |
| piasters | 100 piasters = pound |
| cents | 100 cents = lilangeni, pl., emalangeni |
| sastangs | 100 sastangs = baht |
| millimes | 1000 millimes = dinar |
| seniti | 100 seniti = pa'anga |
| kurus | 100 kurus = lira |

| Currency Name | Country | Major Unit |
|---|---|---|
| | Trinidad & Tobago | dollar |
| Taiwan Dollar | Taiwan, Province of China | new dollar |
| Tanzanian Shilling | Tanzania, United Republic of | shilling |
| Ukraine Hryvnia | Ukraine | hryvnia |
| Uganda Shilling | Uganda | shilling |
| U.S. Dollar | United States, Guam, American Samoa, Marshall Islands, Federated States of Micronesia, Palau, Puerto Rico, Turks & Caicos Islands, U.S.Virgin Islands | dollar |
| Uruguayan Peso | Uruguay | peso uruguay |
| Venezuelan Bolivar | Venezuela | bolivar |
| Vietnamese Dong | Vietnam | new dong |
| Vanuatu Vatu | Vanuatu | vatu |
| Samoan Tala | Samoa | tala |
| CFA Franc BEAC | Cameroon, Central African Republic, Chad, Congo, Equatorial Guinea, Gabon, Guinea Bissau | franc |

| Minor Unit | Equivalence |
|---|---|
| cents | 100 cents = dollar |
| cents | 100 cents = new dollar |
| cents | 100 cents = shilling |
| kopiyka | 100 kopiyka = hryvnia |
| cent | 100 cent = shilling |
| cents | 100 cents = dollar |
| | |
| centésimos | 100 centésimos = peso uruguayo |
| centimos | 100 centimos = bolivar |
| xu, hao | 10 xu = hao, 10 hao = new dong |
| centimes | 100 centimes = vatu |
| sene | 100 sene = tala |
| centimes | 100 centimes = franc |

| Currency Name | Country | Major Unit |
|---|---|---|
| | Anguilla, Antigua & Barbuda, Dominica, Grenada, Montserrat, Saint Kitts & Nevis, Saint Lucia, Saint Vincent &The Grenadines | dollar |
| CFA Franc BCEAO | Benin, Burkina faso, Cote d'Ivoire, Mali, Niger, Senegal, Togo | franc |
| | French Polynesia, New Caledonia, Wallis and Futuna | franc |
| Yugoslav Dinar | Yugoslavia | new dinar |
| South African Rand | South Africa | rand |
| Zambian Kwacha | Zambia | kwacha |
| Zimbabwe Dollar | Zimbabwe | dollar |

| Minor Unit | Equivalence |
| --- | --- |
| cents | 100 cents = dollar |
| centimes | 100 centimes = franc |
| centimes | 100 centimes = franc |
| paras | 100 paras = new dinar |
| cents | 100 cents = rand |
| ngwee | 100 ngwee = kwacha |
| cents | 100 cents = dollar |

## *What is the Euro?*

The euro is the single currency of the European Monetary Union, which was adopted by twelve Member States. (The current membership of the European Union consists of fifteen countries.) Those twelve Member States are Belgium, Germany, Spain, France, Ireland, Italy, Luxembourg, the Netherlands, Austria, Portugal, Finland and Greece.

The name "euro" was chosen by the European Heads of State or Government at the European Council meeting in Madrid in December 1995. Euro bank notes and coins began circulating on January 1, 2002. At that time, all transactions in those countries were valued in Euro, and the "old" notes and coins of these countries were gradually withdrawn from circulation. Today it is accepted in all the member states, and is used just like using the original national currency. However, most outgoing Euro currencies will still be physically convertible for the next several years.

For Americans, the euro has made travel abroad much easier. There is no more currency exchange–which means no more exchange commission to be paid–no more time spent calculating price comparisons, and less time wasted shopping around for the est exchange rate.

Any place that previously used one or more of the Member State currencies now also has adopted the Euro. This applies to territories of Euro-zone countries as well as to places that do not have their own currency. Examples include Andorra, the Canary Islands, French Guyana, Guadeloupe, Martinique, Monaco, and San Marino.

# CHAPTER 6

# MEASUREMENTS FOR THE HOME

## *Temperature: Systems of measurement*

There are three main systems of temperature measurement: Fahrenheit (F), Celsius(C), and Kelvin (K). The following formulas are for converting temperature measurements from one system to another.

## *Formulas*

F C (F-32)/1.8
C F (C x 1.8) + 32
F K (F+459.67)/1.8
KF (Kx1.8)- 459.67
C K C+273.16
KC K-273.16

a = boiling point of water = 212F, 100C, 373.16K
b = freezing point of water = 32F, 0C, 273.16K
c = absolute zero = -459.67F, -273.16C, 0K

## Conversion tables

The table below lists the equivalent units of temperature in Fahrenheit. Celsius, and Kelvin.

### FAHRENHEIT TO CELSIUS TO KELVIN

| F | C | K | F | C | K |
|---|---|---|---|---|---|
| -40.0 | -40 | 233 | -4.0 | -20 | 253 |
| -38.2 | -39 | 234 | -2.2 | -19 | 254 |
| -36.4 | -38 | 235 | -0.4 | -18 | 255 |
| -34.6 | -37 | 236 | 1.4 | -17 | 256 |
| -32.8 | -36 | 237 | 3.2 | -16 | 257 |
| -31.0 | -35 | 238 | 5 | -15 | 258 |
| -29.2 | -34 | 239 | 6.8 | -14 | 259 |
| -27.4 | -33 | 240 | 8.6 | -13 | 260 |
| -25.6 | -32 | 241 | 10.4 | -12 | 261 |
| -23.8 | -31 | 242 | 12.2 | -11 | 262 |
| -22 | -30 | 243 | 14.0 | -10 | 263 |
| -20.2 | -29 | 244 | 15.8 | -9 | 264 |
| -18.4 | -28 | 245 | 17.6 | -8 | 265 |
| -16.6 | -27 | 246 | 19.4 | -7 | 266 |
| -14.8 | -26 | 247 | 21.2 | -6 | 267 |
| -13 | -25 | 248 | 23.0 | -5 | 268 |
| -11.2 | -24 | 249 | 24.8 | -4 | 269 |
| -9.4 | -23 | 250 | 26.6 | -3 | 270 |
| -7.6 | -22 | 251 | 28.4 | -2 | 271 |
| -5.8 | -21 | 252 | 30.2 | -1 | 272 |

| F | C | K | F | C | K |
|---|---|---|---|---|---|
| 2.0 | 0 | 273 | 68.0 | 20 | 293 |
| 3.8 | 1 | 274 | 69.8 | 21 | 294 |
| 5.6 | 2 | 275 | 71.6 | 22 | 295 |
| 7.4 | 3 | 276 | 73.4 | 23 | 296 |
| 9.2 | 4 | 277 | 75.2 | 24 | 297 |
| 1.0 | 5 | 278 | 77.0 | 25 | 298 |
| 2.8 | 6 | 279 | 78.8 | 26 | 299 |
| 4.6 | 7 | 280 | 80.6 | 27 | 300 |
| 6.4 | 8 | 281 | 82.4 | 28 | 301 |
| 8.2 | 9 | 282 | 84.1 | 29 | 302 |
| 0.0 | 10 | 283 | 86.0 | 30 | 303 |
| 1.8 | 11 | 284 | 87.8 | 31 | 304 |
| 3.6 | 12 | 285 | 89.6 | 32 | 305 |
| 5.4 | 13 | 286 | 91.4 | 33 | 306 |
| 7.2 | 14 | 287 | 93.2 | 34 | 307 |
| 9.0 | 15 | 288 | 95.0 | 35 | 308 |
| 0.8 | 16 | 289 | 96.8 | 36 | 309 |
| 2.6 | 17 | 290 | 98.6 | 37 | 310 |
| 4.4 | 18 | 291 | 100.4 | 38 | 311 |
| 6.2 | 19 | 292 | 102.2 | 39 | 312 |

# FAHRENHEIT TO CELSIUS TO KELVIN

| F | C | K | F | C | K |
|---|---|---|---|---|---|
| 104.0 | 40 | 313 | 140.0 | 60 | 333 |
| 105.8 | 41 | 314 | 141.8 | 61 | 334 |
| 107.6 | 42 | 315 | 143.6 | 62 | 335 |
| 109.4 | 43 | 316 | 145.4 | 63 | 336 |
| 111.2 | 44 | 317 | 147.2 | 64 | 337 |
| 113.0 | 45 | 318 | 149.0 | 65 | 338 |
| 114.8 | 46 | 319 | 150.8 | 66 | 339 |
| 116.6 | 47 | 320 | 152.6 | 67 | 340 |
| 118.4 | 48 | 321 | 154.4 | 68 | 341 |
| 120.2 | 49 | 322 | 156.2 | 69 | 342 |
| 122.0 | 50 | 323 | 158.0 | 70 | 343 |
| 123.8 | 51 | 324 | 159.8 | 71 | 344 |
| 125.6 | 52 | 325 | 161.6 | 72 | 345 |
| 127.4 | 53 | 326 | 163.4 | 73 | 346 |
| 129.2 | 54 | 327 | 165.2 | 74 | 347 |
| 131.0 | 55 | 328 | 167.0 | 75 | 348 |
| 132.8 | 56 | 329 | 168.8 | 76 | 349 |
| 134.6 | 57 | 330 | 170.6 | 77 | 350 |
| 136.4 | 58 | 331 | 172.4 | 78 | 351 |
| 138.2 | 59 | 332 | 174.2 | 79 | 352 |

|  | C | K | F | C | K |
|---|---|---|---|---|---|
| 76.0 | 80 | 353 | 212.0 | 100 | 373 |
| 77.8 | 81 | 354 | 213.8 | 101 | 374 |
| 79.6 | 82 | 355 | 215.6 | 102 | 375 |
| 81.4 | 83 | 356 | 217.4 | 103 | 376 |
| 83.2 | 84 | 357 | 219.2 | 104 | 377 |
| 85.0 | 85 | 358 | 221.0 | 105 | 378 |
| 86.8 | 86 | 359 | 222.8 | 106 | 379 |
| 88.6 | 87 | 360 | 224.6 | 107 | 380 |
| 90.4 | 88 | 361 | 226.4 | 108 | 381 |
| 92.2 | 89 | 362 | 228.2 | 109 | 382 |
| 94.0 | 90 | 363 | 230.0 | 110 | 383 |
| 95.8 | 91 | 364 | 231.8 | 111 | 384 |
| 97.6 | 92 | 365 | 233.6 | 112 | 385 |
| 99.4 | 93 | 366 | 235.4 | 113 | 386 |
| 201.2 | 94 | 367 | 237.2 | 114 | 387 |
| 203.0 | 95 | 368 | 239.0 | 115 | 388 |
| 204.8 | 96 | 369 | 240.8 | 116 | 389 |
| 206.6 | 97 | 370 | 242.6 | 117 | 390 |
| 208.4 | 98 | 371 | 244.4 | 118 | 391 |
| 210.2 | 99 | 372 | 246.2 | 119 | 392 |

## A quick temperature reference

| Condition | °F | °C |
|---|---|---|
| Water freezes | 32 | 0 |
| Body temperature | 98.6 | 37 |
| Heat wave | 104 | 40 |
| Water boils | 212 | 100 |

## Cooking

In our everyday life, cooking is probably the single time we think about measurements. Culturally, our use of measurements for cooking borders on the bizarre. While we have different measurements for liquids and solids, they are often referred to by the same terms.

|  | teaspoon | tablespoon | fluid ounce |
|---|---|---|---|
| 1 teaspoon = | 1 | 1/3 | 1/6 |
| 1 tablespoon = | 3 | 1 | 1/2 |
| 1 fluid ounce = | 6 | 2 | 1 |
| 1 gill = | 24 | 8 | 4 |
| 1 cup = | 48 | 16 | 8 |
| 1 pint = | 96 | 32 | 16 |
| 1 quart = | 192 | 64 | 32 |
| 1 gallon = | 768 | 256 | 128 |

## Liquid Measurements

Liquid measurement is not only used for liquids such as water and milk, it is also used when measuring dry and other ingredients such as flour, sugar, shortening, butter, and spices.

| gill | cup | pint | quart | gallon |
|------|------|------|-------|--------|
| 1/24 | * | * | * | * |
| 1/8 | 1/16 | * | * | * |
| 1/4 | 1/8 | 1/16 | * | * |
| 1 | 1/2 | 1/4 | 1/8 | * |
| 2 | 1 | 1/2 | 1/4 | 1/16 |
| 4 | 2 | 1 | 1/2 | 1/0 |
| 8 | 4 | 2 | 1 | 1/4 |
| 32 | 16 | 8 | 4 | 1 |

However, liquid and dry measurements for ingredients are not exactly the same: there are separate liquid and dry measuring cups for a more exact result. The table below shows the differences between dry measurement and liquid measurement:

| Dry Unit | Liquid Unit |
|---|---|
| 1 pint, dry | = 1.1636 pints, liquid |
| 1 quart, dry | = 1.1636 quarts, liquid |
| 1 gallon, dry | = 1.1636 gallons, liquid |

### *Dry Measurements*

Dry measurements are not typically used in recipes; dry measurements are used mainly for measuring fresh produce (e.g. berries are sold by the quart, apples by the bushel). Also, the tiniest cooking measurements are not true measurements at all. For example:

1 pinch = 1/8 teaspoon or less

| | Pint | Quart | Gallon | Peck | Bushel | Cubic Feet |
|---|---|---|---|---|---|---|
| Pint | 1 | 1/2 | 1/8 | 1/16 | 1/64 | 0.019 |
| Quart | 2 | 1 | 1/4 | 1/8 | 1/32 | 0.038 |
| Gallon | 8 | 4 | 1 | 1/2 | 1/8 | 0.155 |
| Peck | 16 | 8 | 2 | 1 | 1/4 | 0.311 |
| Bushel | 64 | 32 | 8 | 4 | 1 | 1.244 |
| Cubic Feet | 51.428 | 25.714 | 6.4285 | 3.2143 | 0.803 | 1 |

## Solid Weight in Cooking

The two most commonly used units of weight measurement for cooking are the ounce and the pound. However, this ounce is not the same as a fluid ounce. In cooking, the rule of thumb is that
16 ounces = 1 pound.

## HANDY MEASURES THAT CONVERT TO METRIC

| Object | U.S. units | Metric |
|---|---|---|
| thimbleful | 30 drops | 2.5 ml |
| 60 drops | 1 teaspoon | 5 ml |
| teaspoon | 1 fl dram | 5 ml |
| dessert spoon | 2 fl drams | 10 ml |
| tablespoon | 4 fl drams | 15 ml |
| 2 tablespoons | 1 fl oz | 30 ml |
| 4 tablespoons | 2 fl oz | 60 ml |
| wine glass | 4 fl oz | 120 ml |
| cup | 8 fl oz | 240 ml |

## Wine Measures
small jigger = 1 fl oz
small wine glass = 2 fl oz
sherry glass = 2 fl oz
cocktail glass = 1/4 pint
large wine glass = 1/4 pint
tumbler = 1/2 pint

## Spirits measures

| | |
|---|---|
| 1 shot = 1 fl oz | 1 fifth = 25.6 shots |
| 1 pony = 1 shot | 1 fifth = 1.6 pints |
| 1 jigger = 1 1/2 shots | 1 fifth = 0.8 quart |
| 1 pint = 16 shots | 1 fifth = 0.758 liter |
| 1 quart = 32 shots | |
| 1 quart = 1 1/4 fifths | |
| 1 magnum of wine= 2 fifths | |
| 1 magnum of wine= 2 bottles | |

## Champagne bottle sizes
| | |
|---|---|
| Nebuchadnezzar | 20 bottles |
| Balthazar | 16 bottles |
| Salamanazar | 12 bottles |
| Methuselah | 8 bottles |
| Rehoboam | 6 bottles |
| Jeroboam | 4 bottles |
| Magnum | 2 bottles |
| Bottle | 750ml or 26 fl oz |

## Oven temperatures

Below is a table of Fahrenheit/Celsius conversions for common oven temperatures.

| Fahrenheit | Celsius | Oven Temperature |
|------------|---------|------------------|
| 225 | 110 | very cool |
| 250 | 130 | |
| 275 | 140 | cool |
| 300 | 150 | |
| 325 | 170 | moderate |
| 350 | 180 | |
| 375 | 190 | moderately hot |
| 400 | 200 | |
| 425 | 220 | hot |
| 450 | 230 | |
| 475 | 240 | very hot |

## *Ingredient's Substitutions*

Even the best-stocked pantry is often missing an ingredient or two. These handy conversions will get your recipe back on track:

| INGREDIENT | QUANTITY |
| --- | --- |
| Baking Powder | 1 tsp double acting |
| Butter | 1 cup |
| Buttermilk | 1 cup |
| Chocolate | 1 ounce |
| Cream | 1 cup |
| Flour, all purpose | 1 cup |
| Flour, cake | 1 cup |
| Honey | 1 cup |
| Milk, fresh whole | 1 cup |
| Molasses | 1 cup |
| Ricotta Cheese | 1 cup |
| Sour Cream | 1 cup |
| Sugar, Brown | 1 cup |
| Sugar, Powdered | 1 1/3 cups |
| Yogurt | 1 cup |

**SUBSTITUTE**

| |
|---|
| 1/4 tsp baking soda + 1/2 cup buttermilk |
| 1 cup margarine |
| 2/3 cup plain yogurt + 1/3 cup sweetened  milk |
| 3 Tbsp cocoa + 1 Tbsp shortening |
| 1/2 cup butter + 3/4 cup milk |
| 1 cup + 2 Tbsp cake flour |
| 7/8 cup all purpose flour |
| 1 1/4 cups sugar + 1/4 cup liquid |
| 1 cup reconstituted dry milk + 2 tsp butter |
| 1 cup honoy |
| 1 cup cottage cheese + 1 Tbsp skim milk |
| 1 cup yogurt |
| 3/4 cup granulated sugar + 1/4 cup molasses |
| 1 cup granulated sugar |
| 1 cup buttermilk |

### *Body measurements*

There are standards in taking body measurements for custom-made clothes, as well as tracking weight loss or weight gain. Here are some tips on taking the most accurate body measurements.

**Neck:** Measure at the fullest part.

**Chest/bust:** Measure at the fullest part of the bust or chest and straight across the back.

**Waist:** Tie a string around the thinnest pall of your waist and leave it there as a point of reference for other measurements.

**Hips:** There are two places to measure hips depending on how you will wear a particular garment: one is 2-4 inches below the waist, at the top of the hipbones: the other is at the fullest pan, usually 7-9 inches below.

**Arm:** Measure at the fullest part, usually about 1 inch below the armpit.

**Arm length:** With the arm slightly bent, tart at the shoulder bone and continue past the elbow to the wrist.

**Back:** Measure from the prominent bone in the back of the neck down the center to the point at which you want the garment to end, e.g. the hips.

# Optimal height/weight measurements

These insurance-company supplied figures tell us what our weight should be for optimal health, depending on our height.

## HEIGHT & WEIGHT TABLE FOR WOMEN

| Height Feet Inches | Small Frame | Medium Frame | Large Frame |
|---|---|---|---|
| 4' 10" | 102-111 | 109-121 | 18-131 |
| 4' 11" | 103-113 | 111-123 | 120-134 |
| 5' 0" | 104-115 | 113-126 | 122-137 |
| 5' 1" | 106-118 | 115-129 | 125-140 |
| 5' 2" | 108-121 | 118-132 | 128-143 |
| 5' 3" | 111-124 | 121-135 | 131-147 |
| 5' 4" | 114-127 | 124-138 | 134-151 |
| 5' 5" | 117-130 | 127-141 | 137-155 |
| 5' 6" | 120-133 | 130-144 | 140-159 |
| 5' 7" | 123-136 | 133-147 | 143-103 |
| 5' 8" | 126-139 | 136-150 | 146-167 |
| 5' 9" | 129-142 | 139-153 | 149-170 |
| 5' 10" | 132-145 | 142-156 | 152-173 |
| 5' 11" | 135-148 | 145-159 | 155-176 |
| 6' 0" | 138-151 | 148-162 | 158-179 |

# HEIGHT & WEIGHT TABLE FOR MEN

| Height Feet Inches | Small Frame | Medium Frame | Large Frame |
|---|---|---|---|
| 5' 2" | 128-134 | 131-141 | 138-150 |
| 5' 3" | 130-136 | 133-143 | 140-153 |
| 5' 4" | 132-138 | 135-145 | 142-156 |
| 5' 5" | 134-140 | 137-148 | 144-160 |
| 5' 6" | 136-142 | 139-151 | 146-164 |
| 5' 7" | 138-145 | 142-154 | 149-168 |
| 5' 8" | 140-148 | 145-157 | 152-172 |
| 5' 9" | 142-151 | 148-160 | 155-176 |
| 5' 10" | 144-154 | 151-163 | 158-180 |
| 5' 11" | 146-157 | 154-166 | 161-184 |
| 6' 0" | 149-160 | 157-170 | 164-188 |
| 6' 1" | 152-164 | 160-174 | 168-192 |
| 6' 2" | 155-168 | 164-178 | 172-197 |
| 6' 3" | 158-172 | 167-182 | 176-202 |
| 6' 4" | 162-176 | 171-187 | 181-207 |

## *Laundry codes*

Most garments contain a label giving cleaning instructions. Usually written, they are often accompanied by a set of symbols that tell you if any item is machine washable and how to wash it. The following are the most common washing instructions.

Machine or hand wash
Can be bleached
Do not bleach
Iron
Do not iron
Dry cleanable
Do not dry clean
Tumble dry
Do not tumble dry

The following chart lists the old and new codes, recommended temperatures (for machine- or hand-washing), and other machine settings, and the types of fabric that should be washed according to that code.

|  | MACHINE WASH | HAND WASH |
|---|---|---|
| Code | Temperature | Temperature |
| 95 | **Very hot**<br>95C (203F)<br>to boil | **Hand hot**<br>50C (122F)<br>or boil |
| 60 | **Hot**<br>60C (140F) | **Hand hot**<br>50C (122F) |
| 50 | **Hand hot**<br>50C (122F) | **Hand hot**<br>50C (122F) |
| 40 | **Warm**<br>40C (104F) | **Warm**<br>40C (104F) |
| 30 | **Cold**<br>30C (86F) | **Cool**<br>30C (86F) |

## *Odds for Casino Games*

### Dice

Odds in dice-throwing are set as a ratio comparing favorable results with unfavorable. With one die, you have six possible results–one for each side of the die; with two die, you have 36 possible results. Some results–a 12 or a 2–you have only one chance to achieve. With these examples, the odds of throwing a 12 or 2 are 35 to 1. For results with two possible combinations, such as a 3, the chances are 35 to 2, or 17 to 1, and so on. The table below shows the odds for each possible combination.

| Combination | Chances |
|-------------|---------|
| 2, 12 | 35-1 |
| 3, 11 | 17-1 |
| 4, 10 | 11-1 |
| 5, 9 | 8.5-1 |
| 6, 8 | 7-1 |
| 7 | 5-1 |

## Odds in Card Games:

### Poker

The odds in poker are determined against a total number of possible combinations of cards equallying 2,598,960. Therefore, the odds of getting a royal flush (4 possible combinations) are 2,598,960 to 4, or 649,739 to 1.

Each of the following poker hands has the related chances:

| | |
|---|---|
| Royal flush: | 649,739 to 1 |
| Straight flush: | 72,192 to 1 |
| Four of a kind: | 4,164 to 1 |
| Full house: | 693 to 1 |
| Flush: | 508 to 1 |
| Straight: | 254 to 1 |
| Three of a kind: | 46 to 1 |
| Two pairs: | 20 to 1 |
| One pair: | 2.4 to 1 |
| Nil: | 2 to 1 |

## Blackjack

There exists the possibility of 1,326 combinations in blackjack; the odds of reaching 21 with two cards from a 52-card deck are 1,326 to 64, or 21 to 1.

| Two-card total | Chances |
|:---:|:---:|
| 21 | 21 to 1 |
| 20 | 9 to 1 |
| 19 | 16.5 to 1 |
| 18 | 15 to 1 |
| 17 | 14 to 1 |
| 16 | 15 to 1 |
| 15 | 14 to 1 |
| 14 | 13 to 1 |
| 13 | 11 to 1 |

# CHAPTER 7

# ENERGY

Energy is the stuff we need to accomplish physical actions. To say it more scientifically, energy refers to a condition or state of a thing: it measures the capability of an object or system to exert a force through a distance on some object.

The SI joule is the standard unit of energy in electronics and general scientific applications. One joule is defined as the amount of energy exerted when a force of one newton is applied over a displacement of one meter.

One joule is the equivalent of one watt of power radiated or dissipated for one second. In some applications, the British thermal unit (Btu) is used to express energy. One Btu is equivalent to approximately 1055 joules.

There are a number of ways in which something can possess energy, each of which corresponds to a different form of energy. There are nine primary ways that an object or a system can possess energy.

### Kinetic Energy

When something is in motion it is said to have kinetic energy. A baseball flying through the air is said to have "kinetic energy" by virtue of the fact that its in motion relative to the ground. You can see that it is has energy because it can impact an object on the ground if it collides with it (either by pushing on it and/or damaging it during the collision). For an object that is moving the kinetic energy equals one half times the mass of the object times the square of the speed of the object. The formula for kinetic energy is:

$EK = (1/2)mv2$
m = mass
v = velocity

## Earthquakes

Earthquakes are pure kinetic energy. Their magnitude is measured in units on the Richter scale, which measures the amount of energy released. The intensity of an earthquake is measured on the Mercalli scale; the numbers refer to an earthquake's effect at a specific place. Below are the various levels of the Mercalli scale and their characteristics:

| No. | Characteristic |
| --- | --- |
| I | instrumental (detected only by seismograph) |
| II | feeble (noticed by people at rest) |
| III | slight (similar to vibrations from a passing truck) |
| IV | moderate (felt indoors, parked cars would rock) |
| V | rather strong (ability to wake sleeping individuals) |
| VI | strong (trees sway, some structural damage caused) |
| VII | very strong (general alarm, walls could crack) |
| VIII | destructive (walls collapse) |
| IX | ruinous (some houses collapse, ground cracks) |
| X | disastrous (buildings destroyed, rails bend) |
| XI | very disastrous (landslides, few buildings would survive) |
| XII | catastrophic (total destruction) |

The following lists the Mercalli and Richter scales, with equivalents in joules.

| Mercalli | Richter | Joules |
|---|---|---|
| I | <3.5 | $<1.6 \times 10^7$ J |
| II | 3.5 | $1.6 \times 10^7$ J |
| III | 4.2 | $7.5 \times 10^8$ J |
| IV | 4.5 | $4.0 \times 10^9$ J |
| V | 4.8 | $2.1 \times 10^{10}$ J |
| VI | 5.4 | $5.7 \times 10^{11}$ J |
| VII | 6.1 | $2.8 \times 10^{12}$ J |
| VIII | 6.5 | $2.5 \times 10^{14}$ J |
| IX | 6.9 | $2.3 \times 10^{15}$ J |
| X | 7.3 | $2.1 \times 10^{16}$ J |
| XI | 8.1 | $1.7 \times 10^{18}$ J |
| XII | >8.1 | $>1.7 \times 10^{18}$ J |

## Potential Energy

A book sitting on a table is said to have "potential energy" because if it is nudged off, gravity will accelerate the book, thereby giving the book kinetic energy. Because the Earth's gravity is necessary to create this kinetic energy, and because this gravity depends on the Earth being present, we say that the "Earth-book relationship is what really possesses this potential energy, and that this energy is converted into kinetic energy as the book falls.

## Thermal energy

Temperature is really a measure of how much thermal energy something has. The higher the temperature, the faster the molecules are moving around or vibrating, and the more kinetic energy the molecules have. Therefore, a hot cup of coffee is said to possess thermal energy. This energy is the collective, microscopic, kinetic and potential energy of the molecules in the coffee.

## Electrical Energy

All matter is made up of atoms. Atoms are made up of smaller particles, called protons (which have positive charge), neutrons (which have neutral charge), and electrons (which are negatively charged). Electrons orbit around the center, or nucleus, of atoms, just like the moon orbits the earth. The nucleus is made up of neutrons and protons.

Some material, particularly metals, have certain electrons that are only loosely attached to their atoms. They can easily be made to move from one atom to another if an electric field is applied to them. When those electrons move among the atoms of matter, a current of electricity is created.

When you apply voltage to a piece of wire. The electrons pass from atom to atom, pushed by the electric field, creating an electrical current. The measure of how well something conducts electricity is called its

conductivity. The recipricol, or oppostite force of conductivity is called the resistance.

## Electromagnetic Energy

Light may be thought of as a pure form of energy. In
scientific terms, any source of light is referred to as
"electromagnetic radiation" in that it is always comprised of little packets of energy called photons.
Photons are created when electrons jump to lower
energy levels in atoms. Photons are absorbed when
electrons jump to higher levels. Photons are also created when a charged particle, such as an electron or
proton, is accelerated. An example of this would be a
radio transmitter antenna.

In addition to being a packet of energy, each photon also has a specific frequency and wavelength associated with it, which depends on how much energy
the photon has. The lower the energy, the longer the
wavelength and lower the frequency. For example, the
reason that sunlight can damage your skin is because
it contains "ultraviolet light," which consists of high
energy photons. These photons have short wavelength and high frequency, and pack enough energy
in each photon to cause physical damage. Radio
waves, and the radiant heat you feel at a distance from
a campfire, for example, are also forms of electromagnetic radiation, or light, except that they consist of low
energy photons that your eyes can't perceive.

## *Measuring energy with the electromagnetic spectrum*

Light, radio waves, and other forms of energy are transmitted through space as electromagnetic waves. These waves have alternating high and low points, similar to the waves in an ocean. The distance between wave crests is called the wavelength, which is measured in meters.

Frequency refers to the number of waves per second passing a certain point, and is measured in hertz (Hz). The electromagnetic spectrum demonstrates the different forms of energy in order of frequency and wavelength.

The following lists the various portion of the electromagnetic spectrum, in order from lowest to highest frequency:

**Radio waves:** transmit television and radio signals

**Radar and microwaves:** radar waves bounce off objects, allowing unseen objects to be seen. Microwaves can cook food quickly.

**Infrared waves:** emitted by all hot objects.

**Visible light:** the band of colored light: red, orange, yellow, green, blue, indigo, and violet.

**Ultraviolet light:** these waves produce vitamin D and cause skin to tan. However, exposure to larger amounts can damage living cells.

**X-rays:** used to internally photograph the structures of the body.

**Gamma rays:** emitted during the decay of some radioisotopes. They can be damaging to the body.

**Cosmic rays:** are caused by nuclear explosions and reactions in space. Nearly all of these waves are absorbed by the Earth's atmosphere.

## Sound Energy

Sound waves are compression waves associated with the potential and kinetic energy of air molecules. When an object moves quickly it compresses the air nearby, giving that air potential energy. That air then expands, transforming the potential energy into kinetic energy (moving air). The moving air pushes on and compresses other air, which can produce a noise. An easy way to remember the process of sound waves is to think of it as "shimmering air."

## Decibels

The loudness of a sound is measured by the size of its vibrations, which is measured in decibels (dB). The dB scale is relative and increases exponentially, beginning with the smallest sound change that can be heard by humans (0-1 dB). A 20 dB sound is 10 times louder than a 10 dB sound: a 30 dB sound is 100 times as loud. Noises at the level of 120-130 dB can cause actual pain; higher levels can cause permanent ear damage. The dB ratings of some common noises are listed below:

**0 dB:** minimum audibility
**30 dB:** soft whisper at 15 ft
**50 dB:** noise outside can be heard inside a home
**55 dB:** light traffic at 50 ft
**60 dB:** normal speaking voice at 3 ft
**85 dB:** pneumatic drill at 50 ft
**90 dB:** heavy traffic at 50 ft
**100 dB:** loud shout at 50 ft
**105 dB:** airplane take-off at 2,000 ft
**117 dB:** noise level of a full-volume disco
**120 dB:** airplane take-off at 200 ft
**130 dB:** pain threshold for humans
**140 dB:** airplane take-off at 100 ft

## Chemical Energy

Chemical energy occurs within an object. For example, think about the reactions that occur within your body. The blood sugar in your body is said to have "chemical energy" because the glucose releases energy when chemically reacts with oxygen. Your muscles use this energy to generate mechanical force and also heat.

Chemical energy is really a form of microscopic potential energy, which exists because of the electric and magnetic forces of attraction exerted between the different parts of each molecule. These parts get rearranged in chemical reactions, releasing or adding to this potential energy.

### *What is a Calorie?*

A calorie is a unit of energy. We tend to associate calories with food, but they apply to anything containing energy. For example, a gallon of gasoline contains about 31,000,000 calories.

Specifically, a calorie is the amount of energy it takes to raise the temperature of 1 gram of water 1 degree. One calorie is equal to 4.184 joules. The calories on a food package are actually kilocalories (1,000 calories = 1 kilocalorie). A food calorie contains 4,184 joules.

In order for us all to survive, we need a constant source of energy. We acquire this energy from food. The number of calories in food is a measure of how much potential energy that food possesses.

For example, a gram of carbohydrates has 4 calories, a gram of protein has 4 calories, and a gram of fat has 9 calories. Foods are a compilation of these three building blocks. So if you know how many carbohydrates, fats, and proteins are in any food, you know how many calories, or how much energy, that food contains.

Our bodies "burn" the calories through a metabolic processes, by which enzymes break the carbohydrates into glucose and other sugars, the fats into glycerol and fatty acids, and the proteins into amino acids. These molecules are then transported through the bloodstream to the cells, where they are either absorbed for immediate use or sent on to the final stage of metabolism in which they are reacted with oxygen to release their stored energy.

## Your Caloric Needs

Just how many calories do our cells need to function? The number is different for every person. 2,000 calories is a rough average of what a person needs to eat in a day, but your body might need more or less. Height, weight, gender, age, and activity level all affect your caloric needs. There are three main factors involved in calculating how many calories your body needs per day:

Basal metabolic rate
Physical activity
Thermic effect of food

Your basal metabolic rate (BMR) is the amount of energy your body needs to function at rest. In general, men have a higher BMR than women. One of the most accurate methods of estimating your basal metabolic rate is the following Harris-Benedict formula:

Adult male: 66 + (6.3 x body weight in lbs.) + (12.9 x height in inches) - (6.8 x age in years)

Adult female: 655 + (4.3 x weight in lbs.) + (4.7 x height in inches) - (4.7 x age in years)

The second factor in the equation, physical activity, consumes the next highest number of calories. Physical activity includes everything from making your bed to jogging. The number of calories you burn in any given activity depends on your body weight. Usually, men use more calories than women for all activities because men often weigh more, and women usually have more body fat and need less energy to retain body heat.

The following chart gives examples of different exercises and the calories burned for a variety of body weights:

| Activity (one hour) | 130lbs | 155lbs | 190lbs |
|---|---|---|---|
| Aerobics, general | 354 | 422 | 518 |
| Automobile repair | 177 | 211 | 259 |
| Backpacking | 413 | 493 | 604 |
| Basketball, shooting baskets | 266 | 317 | 388 |
| Bicycling, <10mph, leisure | 236 | 281 | 345 |
| Bicycling, >20mph, racing | 944 | 1126 | 1380 |
| Calisthenics (pushups, sit-ups), vigorous effort | 472 | 563 | 690 |
| Calisthenics, home, light/moderate effort | 266 | 317 | 388 |
| Carpentry, general | 207 | 246 | 302 |
| Cleaning house | 207 | 246 | 302 |
| Dancing | 266 | 317 | 388 |
| Golf, general | 236 | 281 | 345 |
| Health club exercise | 325 | 387 | 474 |
| Mowing lawn | 325 | 387 | 474 |
| Race walking | 384 | 457 | 561 |
| Shoveling snow, by hand | 354 | 422 | 518 |
| Softball or baseball, fast or slow pitch | 295 | 352 | 431 |
| Stretching, hatha yoga | 236 | 281 | 345 |
| Walk/run-playing moderate | 236 | 281 | 345 |

The thermic effect of food is the third factor in how your body burns calories. This is the amount of energy your body uses to digest the food you eat. To calculate the number of calories you expend in this process, multiply the total number of calories you eat in a day by 0.10, or 10 percent.

The total number of calories a body needs in a day is then the sum of these three calculations. Lots of people wonder if it matters where their calories come from. At its most basic, if we eat exactly the number of calories that we burn and if we're only talking about weight, the answer is no–a calorie is a calorie. A protein calorie is no different from a fat calorie–they are simply units of energy. As long as you burn what you eat, you will maintain your weight; and as long as you burn more than you eat, you'll lose weight.

But when it comes to nutrition, it definitely matters where those calories originate. Carbohydrates and proteins are healthier sources of calories than fats. Although our bodies do need a certain amount of fat to function properly, an excess of fat can have serious health consequences. The U.S. Food and Drug Administration recommends that a maximum of 30 percent of our daily calories come from fat. So, if you eat 2,000 calories a day, that's a maximum of 600 calories from fat, or 67 grams of fat, per day.

# Calorie/joule energy conversion

The following are the factors for converting units of energy from one measuring system to another. There are two kinds of factors are given: quick, for an approximate conversion, and accurate, for an exact conversion.

## CALORIES (CAL)
## JOULES (J)

|        | Quick | Accurate |
|--------|-------|----------|
| cal  J | × 4   | × 4.187  |
| J  cal | ÷ 4   | × 0.239  |

## KILOCALORIES (KCAL)
## KILOJOULES (KJ)

|          | Quick | Accurate |
|----------|-------|----------|
| kcal  kJ | × 4   | × 4.187  |
| kJ  kcal | ÷ 4   | × 0.239  |

## Conversion tables

The tables below can be used to convert units of energy from one measuring system to another.

| Joules to Calories | | Kilojoules to Kilocalories | |
|---|---|---|---|
| J | cal | kJ | kcal |
| 1 | 0.239 | 1 | 0.239 |
| 2 | 0.478 | 2 | 0.478 |
| 3 | 0.716 | 3 | 0.716 |
| 4 | 0.955 | 4 | 0.955 |
| 5 | 1.194 | 5 | 1.194 |
| 6 | 1.433 | 6 | 1.433 |
| 7 | 1.672 | 7 | 1.672 |
| 8 | 1.911 | 8 | 1.911 |
| 9 | 2.150 | 9 | 2.150 |
| 10 | 2.388 | 10 | 2.388 |
| 20 | 4.777 | 20 | 4.777 |
| 30 | 7.165 | 30 | 7.165 |
| 40 | 9.554 | 40 | 9.554 |
| 50 | 11.942 | 50 | 11.942 |
| 60 | 14.330 | 60 | 14.330 |
| 70 | 16.719 | 70 | 16.719 |
| 80 | 19.108 | 80 | 19.108 |
| 90 | 21.496 | 90 | 21.496 |
| 100 | 23.885 | 100 | 23.885 |

| Calories to Joules | | Kilocalories to Kilojoules | |
|---|---|---|---|
| cal | J | kcal | kJ |
| 1 | 4.187 | 1 | 4.187 |
| 2 | 8.374 | 2 | 8.374 |
| 3 | 12.560 | 3 | 12.560 |
| 4 | 16.747 | 4 | 16.747 |
| 5 | 20.934 | 5 | 20.934 |
| 6 | 25.121 | 6 | 25.121 |
| 7 | 29.308 | 7 | 2.9308 |
| 8 | 33.494 | 8 | 33.494 |
| 9 | 37.681 | 9 | 37.681 |
| 10 | 41.868 | 10 | 41.868 |
| 20 | 83.736 | 20 | 83.736 |
| 30 | 125.604 | 30 | 125.604 |
| 40 | 167.472 | 40 | 167.472 |
| 50 | 209.340 | 50 | 209.340 |
| 60 | 251.208 | 60 | 251.208 |
| 70 | 293.076 | 70 | 293.076 |
| 80 | 334.944 | 80 | 334.944 |
| 90 | 376.812 | 90 | 376.812 |
| 100 | 418.680 | 100 | 418.680 |

## Electrochemical Energy

The energy stored in a battery is contained in a chemical way. But electricity is also involved, so we say that the battery stores "electrochemical energy."

## Nuclear Energy

The sun, the interior of the Earth, and nuclear reactors all have "nuclear reactions" as the source of their energy: their reactions involve changes in the structure of the nuclei of atoms. In the sun, hydrogen nuclei combine to make helium nuclei in a process called fusion, which releases energy. In the interior of the Earth, or modelled in a nuclear reactor, uranium nuclei split apart in a process called fission. In fact, in both cases, fusion or fission, some of the matter making up the nuclei is actually converted into energy.

# CHAPTER 8

# SPEED

Speed is always a relationship between time and distance, measured as a "rate": what is the fastest time it takes to get from here to there. The following chapter breaks down various lengths and converts U.S. units to metric units.

## Formulas

The following are the factors for converting units of speed from one measuring system to another. There are two kinds of factors are given: quick, for an approximate conversion, and accurate, for an exact conversion.

|  | Quick | Accurate |
|---|---|---|
| **MILES PER HOUR (MPH)** | | |
| **KILOMETERS PER HOUR (KM/H)** | | |
|       mph  km/h | × 1.5 | × 1.609 |
|       km/h  mph | ÷ 1.5 | × 0.621 |
| **YARDS PER MINUTE (YPM)** | | |
| **METERS PER MINUTE (M/MIN)** | | |
|       ypm  m/min | ÷ 1 | × 0.914 |
|       m/min  ypm | × 1 | × 1.094 |
| **FEET PER MINUTE (FT/MIN)** | | |
| **METERS PER MINUTE (M/MIN)** | | |
|       ft/min  m/min | ÷ 3 | × 0.305 |
|       m/min  ft/min | × 3 | × 3.281 |
| **M INCHES PER SECOND (IN/S)** | | |
| **CENTIMETERS PER SECOND (CM/S)** | | |
|       in/s  cm/s | × 2.5 | × 2.54 |
|       cm/s  in/s | ÷ 2.5 | × 0.394 |

|  | | Quick | Accurate |
|---|---|---|---|
| INTERNATIONAL KNOTS (KN) | | | |
| MILES PER HOUR (MPH) | | | |
| kn  mph | | × 1 | × 1.151 |
| mph  kn | | ÷ 1 | × 0.869 |
| INTERNATIONAL KNOTS (KN) | | | |
| KILOMETERS PER HOUR (KM/H) | | | |
| kn  km/h | | × 2 | × 1.852 |
| km/h  kn | | ÷ 2 | × 0.540 |
| MILES PER HOUR (MPH) | | | |
| FEET PER SECOND (FT/S) | | | |
| mph  ft/s | | × 1.5 | × 1.467 |
| ft/s  mph | | ÷ 1.5 | × 0.682 |
| KILOMETERS PER HOUR (KM/H) | | | |
| METERS PER SECOND (M/S) | | | |
| km/h  m/s | | ÷ 3.5 | × 0.278 |
| m/s  km/h | | × 3.5 | × 3.599 |

## Conversion tables

The tables below can be used to convert units of speed. The first group of tables converts U.S. units to metric, and vice versa. The second group converts knots and metric units.

| Miles per hour to Kilometers per hour | | Kilometers per hour to Miles per hour | |
|---|---|---|---|
| mph | km/h | km/h | mph |
| 1 | 1.609 | 1 | 0.621 |
| 2 | 3.219 | 2 | 1.242 |
| 3 | 4.828 | 3 | 1.864 |
| 4 | 6.437 | 4 | 2.485 |
| 5 | 8.047 | 5 | 3.106 |
| 6 | 9.656 | 6 | 3.728 |
| 7 | 11.265 | 7 | 4.349 |
| 8 | 12.875 | 8 | 4.970 |
| 9 | 14.484 | 9 | 5.592 |
| 10 | 16.093 | 10 | 6.213 |
| 20 | 32.187 | 20 | 12.427 |
| 30 | 48.280 | 30 | 18.641 |
| 40 | 64.374 | 40 | 24.854 |
| 50 | 80.467 | 50 | 31.068 |
| 60 | 96.561 | 60 | 37.282 |
| 70 | 112.654 | 70 | 43.495 |
| 80 | 128.748 | 80 | 49.709 |
| 90 | 144.841 | 90 | 55.923 |
| 100 | 160.934 | 100 | 62.137 |

| Yards per minute to Meters per minute | | Meters per minute to Yards per minute | |
|---|---|---|---|
| ypm | m/min | m/min | ypm |
| 1 | 0.914 | 1 | 1.094 |
| 2 | 1.829 | 2 | 2.187 |
| 3 | 2.743 | 3 | 3.281 |
| 4 | 3.658 | 4 | 4.374 |
| 5 | 4.572 | 5 | 5.468 |
| 6 | 5.486 | 6 | 6.562 |
| 7 | 6.401 | 7 | 7.655 |
| 8 | 7.315 | 8 | 8.749 |
| 9 | 8.230 | 9 | 9.842 |
| 10 | 9.144 | 10 | 10.936 |
| 20 | 18.288 | 20 | 21.872 |
| 30 | 27.432 | 30 | 32.808 |
| 40 | 36.576 | 40 | 43.744 |
| 50 | 45.720 | 50 | 54.680 |
| 60 | 54.864 | 60 | 65.616 |
| 70 | 64.008 | 70 | 76.552 |
| 80 | 73.152 | 80 | 87.488 |
| 90 | 82.296 | 90 | 98.424 |
| 100 | 91.440 | 100 | 109.360 |

| Feet per minute to Meters per minute | | Meters per minute to Feet per minute | |
|---|---|---|---|
| min | m/min | min | ft/min |
| 1 | 0.305 | 1 | 3.281 |
| 2 | 0.610 | 2 | 6.562 |
| 3 | 0.914 | 3 | 9.842 |
| 4 | 1.219 | 4 | 13.123 |
| 5 | 1.524 | 5 | 16.404 |
| 6 | 1.829 | 6 | 19.685 |
| 7 | 2.134 | 7 | 22.966 |
| 8 | 2.438 | 8 | 26.246 |
| 9 | 2.743 | 9 | 29.527 |
| 10 | 3.048 | 10 | 32.808 |
| 20 | 6.096 | 20 | 65.616 |
| 30 | 9.144 | 30 | 98.424 |
| 40 | 12.192 | 40 | 131.232 |
| 50 | 15.240 | 50 | 164.040 |
| 60 | 18.288 | 60 | 196.848 |
| 70 | 21.336 | 70 | 229.656 |
| 80 | 24.384 | 80 | 262.464 |
| 90 | 27.432 | 90 | 295.272 |
| 100 | 30.480 | 100 | 328.080 |

| Inches per second to Centimeters per second | | Centimeters per second to Inches per second | |
|---|---|---|---|
| in/s | cm/s | cm/s | in/s |
| 1 | 2.54 | 1 | 0.394 |
| 2 | 5.08 | 2 | 0.787 |
| 3 | 7.62 | 3 | 1.181 |
| 4 | 10.16 | 4 | 1.579 |
| 5 | 12.70 | 5 | 1.969 |
| 6 | 15.24 | 6 | 2.362 |
| 7 | 17.78 | 7 | 2.760 |
| 8 | 20.32 | 8 | 3.150 |
| 9 | 22.86 | 9 | 3.543 |
| 10 | 25.40 | 10 | 3.937 |
| 20 | 50.80 | 20 | 7.874 |
| 30 | 76.20 | 30 | 11.811 |
| 40 | 101.60 | 40 | 15.748 |
| 50 | 127.00 | 50 | 10.085 |
| 60 | 162.40 | 60 | 23.622 |
| 70 | 177.80 | 70 | 27.559 |
| 80 | 203.20 | 80 | 31.496 |
| 90 | 228.60 | 90 | 35.433 |
| 100 | 254.00 | 100 | 39.370 |

| International knots to Miles per hour | | Miles per hour to International knots | |
|---|---|---|---|
| kn | mph | mph | kn |
| 1 | 1.151 | 1 | 0.869 |
| 2 | 2.302 | 2 | 1.738 |
| 3 | 3.452 | 3 | 2.607 |
| 4 | 4.603 | 4 | 3.476 |
| 5 | 5.753 | 5 | 4.345 |
| 6 | 6.905 | 6 | 5.214 |
| 7 | 8.055 | 7 | 6.083 |
| 8 | 9.206 | 8 | 6.952 |
| 9 | 10.357 | 9 | 7.821 |
| 10 | 11.508 | 10 | 8.690 |
| 20 | 23.016 | 20 | 17.380 |
| 30 | 34.523 | 30 | 26.069 |
| 40 | 46.031 | 40 | 34.759 |
| 50 | 57.540 | 50 | 43.449 |
| 60 | 69.047 | 60 | 52.139 |
| 70 | 80.555 | 70 | 60.828 |
| 80 | 92.062 | 80 | 69.518 |
| 90 | 103.570 | 90 | 78.208 |
| 100 | 115.078 | 100 | 86.898 |

| International knots to Kilometers per hour | | Kilometers per hour to knots | |
|---|---|---|---|
| kn | km/h | km/h | kn |
| 1 | 1.852 | 1 | 0.540 |
| 2 | 3.704 | 2 | 1.08 |
| 3 | 5.556 | 3 | 1.62 |
| 4 | 7.408 | 4 | 2.16 |
| 5 | 9.260 | 5 | 2.70 |
| 6 | 11.112 | 6 | 3.23 |
| 7 | 12.964 | 7 | 3.77 |
| 8 | 14.816 | 8 | 4.31 |
| 9 | 16.668 | 9 | 4.85 |
| 10 | 18.520 | 10 | 5.30 |
| 20 | 37.040 | 20 | 10.78 |
| 30 | 55.560 | 30 | 16.17 |
| 40 | 74.080 | 40 | 21.56 |
| 50 | 92.600 | 50 | 26.95 |
| 60 | 111.120 | 60 | 32.34 |
| 70 | 129.640 | 70 | 37.73 |
| 80 | 148.160 | 80 | 43.12 |
| 90 | 166.680 | 90 | 48.51 |
| 100 | 185.200 | 100 | 53.90 |

| Miles per hour to Feet per second | | Feet per second to Miles per hour | |
|---|---|---|---|
| mph | ft/s | ft/s | mph |
| 1 | 1.467 | 1 | 0.682 |
| 2 | 2.933 | 2 | 1.364 |
| 3 | 4.400 | 3 | 2.046 |
| 4 | 5.867 | 4 | 2.728 |
| 5 | 7.334 | 5 | 3.410 |
| 6 | 8.800 | 6 | 4.092 |
| 7 | 10.267 | 7 | 4.774 |
| 8 | 11.734 | 8 | 5.456 |
| 9 | 13.203 | 9 | 6.138 |
| 10 | 14.667 | 10 | 6.820 |
| 20 | 29.334 | 20 | 13.640 |
| 30 | 44.001 | 30 | 20.460 |
| 40 | 58.668 | 40 | 27.280 |
| 50 | 73.335 | 50 | 34.100 |
| 60 | 88.002 | 60 | 40.920 |
| 70 | 102.669 | 70 | 47.74 |
| 80 | 117.336 | 80 | 54.56 |
| 90 | 132.003 | 90 | 61.380 |
| 100 | 146.670 | 100 | 68.200 |

| Kilometers per hour to Meters per second | | Meters per second to Kilometers per hour | |
|---|---|---|---|
| km/h | m/s | m/s | km/h |
| 1 | 0.278 | 1 | 3.599 |
| 2 | 0.556 | 2 | 7.198 |
| 3 | 0.834 | 3 | 10.797 |
| 4 | 1.111 | 4 | 14.396 |
| 5 | 1.389 | 5 | 17.995 |
| 6 | 1.669 | 6 | 21.594 |
| 7 | 1.945 | 7 | 25.193 |
| 8 | 2.222 | 8 | 28.792 |
| 9 | 2.500 | 9 | 32.391 |
| 10 | 2.778 | 10 | 35.990 |
| 20 | 5.556 | 20 | 71.980 |
| 30 | 8.334 | 30 | 107.970 |
| 40 | 11.112 | 40 | 143.960 |
| 50 | 13.890 | 50 | 179.950 |
| 60 | 16.668 | 60 | 215.940 |
| 70 | 19.446 | 70 | 251.930 |
| 80 | 22.224 | 80 | 287.920 |
| 90 | 25.002 | 90 | 323.910 |
| 100 | 27.780 | 100 | 359.900 |

## World's Fastest Records

The following are examples of record-holding speeds. How do you measure up?

**World's fastest train:** 1997: The bullet train Shinkansen services Osaka and Hakata, Japan. It can travel 186 miles (or 300 kilometers) per hour.

**World's fastest car:** 1997: The world's fastest car, the Thrust SSC, holds the world land speed record. Designed by Ron Ayres, the car is a twin jet-propelled supersonic car that can break the sound barrier at 76: miles per hour, or 1,220.8km/h.

**Fastest plane:** 1964: Developed for the U.S.AF nearly 40 years ago, SR-71s remains the world's fastest and highest-flying production aircraft. The aircraft flew more than 2200 miles per hour (Mach 3+ or more than three times the speed of sound).

**Fastest bicycle time:** 1995: Fred Rompelberg of The Netherlands achieved a speed of 268.831 miles per hour at the Bonneville Salt Flats in Utah.

## What's a Mach?

A Mach is a number named for Austrian physicist and philosopher, Ernst Mach, that measures the speed of an object relative to the speed of sound. Mach 1 equals the speed of sound. Sound travels at 331 miles per second, or 740 mph. An aircraft traveling at Mach 2 is traveling at twice the speed of sound.

# CHAPTER 9

# OUR PLANET EARTH

The world we inhabit is thought to be about 4.55 billion years old, just about one-third of the 13-billion-year age estimated for the universe. The total area of the planet is 510.072 million sq km, which break down to the following figures:

**land:** 148.94 million sq km
**water:** 361.132 million sq km

This chapter covers a variety of fun facts about the Earth.

### Earth's interior

The Earth is made of various layers, working from the outside inward. They are as follows:

**Crust** (beginning under the oceans) 4 miles (6 km) deep; made of basalt (a type of rock). The continental crust averages 22 miles (35 km) deep; made of granite.

**Mantle** 1,810 miles (2,912 km) deep: probably containing peridotite, dunite, and ecologite.

**Outer core** 1,242 miles (1,999 km) deep; probably liquid iron with some dissolved sulfur and silicon.

Inner core 842 miles (1,354 km) deep; probably solid iron.

### Earth's atmospheric levels

**Exosphere:** (traces of hydrogen), up to 5.000 miles (8,000 km)

**Thermosphere:** up to 220 miles (350 km)

**Mesosphere:** to 50 miles (80 km) above the Earth's surface.

**Stratosphere:** to about 30 miles (50 km) above the Earth's surface.

**Troposphere:** up to 5 miles (8 km) above the Earth at the poles, 8 miles (13 km) at the Equator.

Sea level: the lowest astmospheric level.

## Climate

The climate of any region is primarily the result of its relationship to the Equator, specifically, its latitude and longitude. Other factors that affect climate include altitude and its relationship to sea level; the air pressure; the wind patterns; and the rainfall. Climate zones are banded horizontally across the Earth in three predominant categories:

**Polar climate zones:** The polar regions are perpetually covered by snow and ice. In these high latitude regions, the sun is never high enough in the sky to cause appreciable melting and the temperature rarely rises above freezing. Long polar nights can last up to six months without appreciable sunshine. Oddly, polar climates tend to be dry because the descending air is cold and lacks significant moisture, precluding the formation of clouds and snowfall. Some polar regions receive less than 10 inches of precipitation each year, and can be as dry as the hottest deserts.

**Temperate climate zones:** Temperate climates are those without extremes temperature changes, and usually have moderate precipitation. These climate zones are between 50∞ to 60∞ north and south of the Equator. Precipitation tends to develop along warm and cold fronts, where cold air from the polar easterly winds forces the warm, moist air of the westerly winds to rise, which, on cooling, releases the moisture as clouds and ultimately rain or snow.

**Tropical climate zone:** Centered on the equator is the tropical or equatorial zone, a belt of relatively low atmospheric pressure and heavy rainfall, due to the rising air. Historically, the zone was known to sailors as the Doldrums because, with the very light winds, ships would often spend many weeks stuck at sea.

## *The Continents*

The land masses of the seven continents are as follows:

| land mass | Square miles | Square kilometers |
|---|---|---|
| Africa: | 11,685,000 | 30,264,000 |
| Asia: | 17,085,000 | 44,250,000 |
| Antarctica: | 5,100,000 | 13,209,000 |
| Australasia: | 3,295,000 | 8,534,000 |
| Europe: | 3,825,000 | 9,907,000 |
| North America: | 9,420,000 | 24,398,000 |
| South America: | 6,870,000 | 17,793,000 |

## OCEANS AND SEAS

| Body of water | miles | kilometers |
|---|---|---|
| Pacific Ocean | 63,800,000 | 165,242,000 |
| Atlantic Ocean | 31,800,000 | 82,362,000 |
| Indian Ocean | 28,400,000 | 73,556,000 |
| Arctic Ocean | 5,400,000 | 13,986,000 |
| South China Sea | 1,149,000 | 2,975,000 |
| Caribbean Sea | 1,063,000 | 2,753,000 |
| Mediterranean Sea | 967,000 | 2,505,000 |

## VOLCANOES AND MOUNTAINS

| Highest volcanoes | feet | meters |
|---|---|---|
| Ojos del Salado, S. America: | 22,590 ft | 6,885 m |
| Pissis, S. America: | 22,580 ft | 6,882 m |
| Llullaillaco, S. America: | 22,110 ft | 6,739 m |
| Chimborazo, S. America: | 20,703 ft | 6,310 m |
| McKinley, N. America: | 20,320 ft | 6,194 m |
| Cotopaxi, S. America: | 19,344 ft | 5,896 m |
| Kilimanjaro, Africa: | 19,340 ft | 5,895 m |
| Antisana, S. America: | 18,892 ft | 5,758 m |
| Citlaltepetl, N. America: | 18,853 ft | 5,746 m |
| Elbrus, Europe: | 18,480 ft | 5,633 m |

## HIGHEST MOUNTAINS

| Mountain | Feet | Meters |
|---|---|---|
| Everest, Himalayas | 29,029 ft | 8,848 m |
| K2 (Godwin Austen) Himalayas | 28,251 ft | 8,611 m |
| Kanchenjunga Himalayas | 28,208 ft | 8,598 m |
| Lhotse Himalayas | 27,923 ft | 8,511 m |
| Yalung Kang Himalayas | 27,893 ft | 8,502 m |
| Makalu Himalayas | 27,824 ft | 8,481 m |
| Dhaulagiri Himalayas | 26,811 ft | 8,172 m |
| Manaslu Himalayas | 26,758 ft | 8,156 m |
| Cho Oyu Himalayas | 26,748 ft | 8,153 m |
| Nanga Parbat Himalayas | 26,660 ft | 8.126 m |

## HIGHEST MOUNTAIN ON EACH CONTINENT

| Mountain | Feet | Meters |
|---|---|---|
| Everest, Asia: | 29,029 ft | 8,848 m |
| Aconcagua S. America | 22,834 ft | 6,960 m |
| McKinley N. America | 20,320 ft | 6,194 m |
| Kilimanjaro Africa | 19,340 ft | 5.895 m |
| Elbrus Europe | 18,480 ft | 5,633 m |
| Vinson Massif Antarctica | 16,863 ft | 5,140 m |
| Cook Australasia | 12,349 ft | 3,764 m |

## LONGEST RIVERS

| River | Miles | Kilometers |
|---|---|---|
| Nile, Africa | 4,132 mi | 6,650 km |
| Amazon, S. America | 4,000 mi | 6,437 km |
| Mississippi-Missouri-Red Rock, N. America | 3,860 mi | 6.212 km |
| Ob-Irivsh, Asia | 3.461 mi | 5.570 km |
| Yangtze, Asia | 3,430 mi | 5.520 km |
| Huang He, Asia | 2,903 mi | 4.672 km |
| Congo, Africa | 2,900 mi | 4.667 km |
| Amur, Asia | 2,802 mi | 4.509 km |
| Lena, Asia | 2,653 mi | 4,270 km |
| Mackenzie, N. America | 2,635 mi | 4,241 km |

## LONGEST RIVER ON EACH CONTINENT

| River | Miles | Kilometers |
|---|---|---|
| Nile, Africa | 4,132 ml | 6,650 km |
| Amazon, S. America | 4,000 mi | 6,437 km |
| Mississippi-Missouri-Red Rock, N. America | 3,860 mi | 6,212 km |
| Ob-Irtysh, Asia | 3,461 mi | 5,570 km |
| Volga, Europe | 2,293 mi | 3,690 km |
| Murray, Australasia | 2,000 mi | 3,219 km |

## LARGEST LAKES

| Lake | Square miles | Square Kilometers |
| --- | --- | --- |
| Superior | 31,800 | 82,400 |
| Victoria | 26,800 | 69,500 |
| Huron | 23,000 | 59,600 |
| Michigan | 22,400 | 58,000 |
| Great Bear | 12,300 | 31,800 |
| Bavkal | 12,200 | 31,500 |
| Great Slave | 11,000 | 28,400 |
| Tanganyika | 11,000 | 28,400 |
| Malawi | 10,900 | 28,200 |
| Erie | 9.900 | 25,700 |

## LARGEST WATERFALLS

| Waterfall | Feet | Meters |
| --- | --- | --- |
| Angel, Venezuela | 3,212 ft | 979 m |
| Tugela, S. Africa | 3,110 ft | 948 m |
| Utigard, Norway | 2,625 ft | 800 m |
| Mongefossen, Norway | 2,540 ft | 774 m |
| Yosemite. U.S.A. | 2,425 ft | 739 m |
| Ostre Mardola Foss, Norway | 2,154 ft | 657 m |
| Tyssestrengane, Norway | 2.120 ft | 646 m |
| Kukenaom, Venezuela | 2,000 ft | 610 m |
| Sutherland, N. Zealand | 1,904 ft | 580 m |
| Kjellfossen, Norway | 1,841 ft | 561 m |

## LARGEST DESERTS

| Desert | Square Miles | Square Kilometers |
|---|---|---|
| Sahara | 3,242,000 | 8,397,000 |
| Australian | 598,000 | 1,549,000 |
| Arabian | 502,000 | 1,300,000 |
| Gobi | 401,000 | 1,039,000 |
| Kalahari | 201,000 | 521,000 |
| Turkestan | 139,000 | 360,000 |
| Takla Makan | 124,000 | 321,000 |
| Sonoran | 120,000 | 311,000 |
| Namib | 120,000 | 311,000 |
| Thar | 100,000 | 259,000 |
| Wyoming | 98,000 | 254,000 |

## DEEPEST CAVES

| Cave | Feet | Meters |
|---|---|---|
| Roseau Jean Bernard, France | 5,256 | 1,602 |
| Shakta Pantjukhina, Russian Caucasus | 4,947 | 1,508 |
| Sistema del Trave, Spain | 4,728 | 1,441 |
| San Agustin, Mexico | 4,439 | 1,353 |
| Schwersystem, Austria | 3,999 | 1,219 |
| Abisso Olivifer, Italy | 3,970 | 1,210 |
| Anou Imis, Algeria | 3,802 | 1,159 |
| Siebenhengste System, Switzerland | 3,346 | 1,020 |

### Capitals Across the World

All of the previous data conveyed the natural wonders of the world. The following lists some of man's most important worldly creations. Specifically, we have learned to control our world through the various political systems. The formation of government is an amazing achievement over the natural state of Planet Earth.

The following lists the capitals of the countries of the world, at the time of printing:

| Country | Capital |
| --- | --- |
| Afghanistan | Kabul |
| Albania | Tirana |
| Algeria | Algiers |
| Andorra | Andorra la Vella |
| Angola | Luanda |
| Antigua and Barbuda | St. John's (capital of Antigua); Codrington (capital of Barbuda) |
| Argentina | Buenos Aires |
| Armenia | Yerevan |
| Australia | Canberra |
| Austria | Vienna |
| Azerbaijan | Baku |
| Bahamas | Nassau |

| Country | Capital |
| --- | --- |
| Bahrain | Al-Man·mah |
| Bangladesh | Dhaka |
| Barbados | Bridgetown |
| Belarus | Minsk |
| Belgium | Brussels |
| Belize | Belmopan |
| Benin | Porto-Novo |
| Bhutan | Thimphu |
| Bolivia | La Paz |
| Bosnia and Herzegovina | Sarajevo |
| Botswana | Gaborone |
| Brazil | Brasilia |
| Brunei Darussalam | Bandar Seri Begawan |
| Bulgaria | Sofia |
| Burkina Faso | Ouagadougou |
| Burundi | Bujumbura |
| Cambodia | Phnom Penh |
| Cameroon | Yaoundé |
| Canada | Ottawa |
| Cape Verde | Praia |
| Central African Republic | Bangui |
| Chad | N'Djamena |
| Chile | Santiago |
| China | Beijing |
| Colombia | Santafé de Bogot· |
| Comoros | Moroni |
| Congo | Brazzaville |

| Country | Capital |
|---|---|
| Democratic Republic of the Congo | Kinshasa |
| Costa Rica | San José |
| Côte d'Ivoire | Yamoussoukro |
| Croatia | Zagreb |
| Cuba | Havana |
| Cyprus | Nicosia |
| Czech Republic | Prague |
| Denmark | Copenhagen |
| Djibouti | Djibouti |
| Dominica | Roseau |
| Dominican Republic | Santo Domingo |
| East Timor | Dili |
| Ecuador | Quito |
| Egypt | Cairo |
| El Salvador | San Salvador |
| Equatorial Guinea | Malabo |
| Eritrea | Asmara |
| Estonia | Tallinn |
| Ethiopia | Addis Ababa |
| Fiji | Suva |
| Finland | Helsinki |
| France | Paris |
| Gabon | Libreville |
| The Gambia | Banjul |
| Georgia | Tbilisi |

| Country | Capital |
| --- | --- |
| Germany | Berlin |
| Ghana | Accra |
| Greece | Athens |
| Grenada | St. George's |
| Guatemala | Guatemala City |
| Guinea | Conakry |
| Guinea-Bissau | Bissau |
| Guyana | Georgetown |
| Haiti | Port-au-Prince |
| Honduras | Tegucigalpa |
| Hungary | Budapest |
| Iceland | Reykjavik |
| India | Delhi |
| Indonesia | Jakarta |
| Iran | Tehran |
| Iraq | Baghdad |
| Ireland | Dublin |
| Israel | Jerusalem |
| Italy | Rome |
| Jamaica | Kingston |
| Japan | Tokyo |
| Jordan | Amman |
| Kazakhstan | Astana |
| Kenya | Nairobi |
| Kiribati | Tarawa |
| North Korea | Pyongyang |

| Country | Capital |
|---|---|
| South Korea | Seoul |
| Kuwait | Kuwait City |
| Kyrgyzstan | Bishkek |
| Laos | Vientiane |
| Latvia | Riga |
| Lebanon | Beirut |
| Lesotho | Maseru |
| Liberia | Monrovia |
| Libya | Tripoli |
| Liechtenstein | Vaduz |
| Lithuania | Vilnius |
| Luxembourg | Luxembourg |
| Macedonia | Skopje |
| Madagascar | Antananarivo |
| Malawi | Lilongwe |
| Malaysia | Kuala Lumpur |
| Maldives | Malé |
| Mali | Bamako |
| Malta | Valletta |
| Marshall Islands | Majuro |
| Mauritania | Nouakchott |
| Mauritius | Port Louis |
| Mexico | Mexico City |
| Micronesia | Palikir |
| Moldova | Chisinau |
| Monaco | Monaco |

| Country | Capital |
| --- | --- |
| Mongolia | Ulaan Baatar |
| Morocco | Rabat |
| Mozambique | Maputo |
| Myanmar | Rangoon |
| Namibia | Windhoek |
| Nauru | Yaren |
| Nepal | Kathmandu |
| The Netherlands | Amsterdam |
| New Zealand | Wellington |
| Nicaragua | Managua |
| Niger | Niamey |
| Nigeria | Abuja |
| Norway | Oslo |
| Oman | Muscat |
| Pakistan | Islamabad |
| Palau | Koror |
| Panama | Panama City |
| Papua New Guinea | Port Moresby |
| Paraguay | Asunción |
| Peru | Lima |
| The Philippines | Manila |
| Poland | Warsaw |
| Portugal | Lisbon |
| Qatar | Doha |
| Romania | Bucharest |
| Russia | Moscow |

| Country | Capital |
|---------|---------|
| Rwanda | Kigali |
| St. Kitts and Nevis | Basseterre |
| St. Lucia | Castries |
| St. Vincent and The Grenadines | Kingstown |
| Samoa | Apia |
| San Marino | San Marino |
| São Tomé and Príncipe | São Tomé |
| Saudi Arabia | Riyadh |
| Senegal | Dakar |
| Seychelles | Victoria |
| Sierra Leone | Freetown |
| Singapore | Singapore |
| Slovakia | Bratislava |
| Slovenia | Ljubljana |
| Solomon Islands | Honiara |
| Somalia | Mogadishu |
| South Africa | Pretoria |
| Spain | Madrid |
| Sri Lanka | Colombo |
| Sudan | Khartoum |
| Suriname | Paramaribo |
| Swaziland | Mbabane |
| Sweden | Stockholm |
| Switzerland | Bern |
| Syria | Damascus |

| Country | Capital |
| --- | --- |
| Taiwan | Taipei |
| Tajikistan | Dushanbe |
| Tanzania | Dodoma |
| Thailand | Bangkok |
| Togo | Lomé |
| Tonga | Nukualofa |
| Trinidad and Tobago | Port-of-Spain |
| Tunisia | Tunis |
| Turkey | Ankara |
| Turkmenistan | Ashgabat |
| Tuvalu | Funafuti |
| Uganda | Kampala |
| Ukraine | Kiev |
| United Arab Emirates | Abu Dhabi |
| United Kingdom | London |
| United States | Washington, D.C. |
| Uruguay | Montevideo |
| Uzbekistan | Tashkent |
| Vanuatu | Port Vila |
| Venezuela | Caracas |
| Vietnam | Hanoi |
| Western Sahara | El Aaiun |
| Yemen | Sana· |
| Yugoslavia | Belgrade |
| Zambia | Lusaka |
| Zimbabwe | Harare |

## World's Tallest Buildings

| Building and location |
| --- |
| Shanghai World Financial Center, China |
| Petronas Twin Towers, Malaysia |
| Sears Tower, Chicago |
| Asia Plaza, Kaohsiung, Taiwan |
| Taipei Int'l Finance Centre, Taiwan |
| Jin Mao Building, Shanghai |
| Empire State Building, New York |
| Central Plaza, Hong Kong |
| Bank of China Tower, Hong Kong |

| Year Completed | Stories | Meters | feet |
|---|---|---|---|
| 2004? | 95+ | 460+ | 1,509+ |
| 1998 | 88 | 452 | 1,483 |
| 1974 | 110 | 442 | 1,450 |
| 2008? | 103 | 431 | 1,414 |
| 2008 ? | 101 | 428 | 1,404 |
| 1999 | 88 | 421 | 1,381 |
| 1931 | 02 | 381 | 1,250 |
| 1992 | 78 | 374 | 1,227 |
| 1989 | 70 | 369 | 1,209 |

# CHAPTER 10

# THE REST OF THE UNIVERSE

The mysteries of our universe have not all been discovered. However, as science progresses, we know much more about each of our neighboring planets than ever before.

## Astronomical measurements

The table below lists standard abbreviations and equivalents for the units used in measuring astronomical distances. These are very large units and are related to the Earth's orbit. A light year (ly) is the distance light travels—at its speed of 186.282 mi/s—through space over a tropical year. An astronomical unit (au) is the mean distance between the Earth and the Sun. A parsec (pc) is the distance at which a baseline of 1 au in length subtends an angle of 1 second.

1 au = 93,000,000 mi = 149,600,000 km
1 ly = 5,878,000,000,000 mi = 9,460,500,000,000 km
1 pc = 19,174,000,000,000 mi = 30,857,200,000,000 km
1 ly = 63,240 au
1 pc = 206,265 au = 3.262 ly

## Planetary data

| | Mercury | Venus | Earth |
|---|---|---|---|
| Mean distance from Sun | 0.39 au | 0.72 au | 1.00 au |
| Distance at perihelion | 0.31 au | 0.72 au | 0.98 au |
| Distance at aphelion | 0.47 au | 0.73 au | 1.02 au |
| Closest distance to Earth | 0.54 au | 0.27 au | |
| Average orbital speed | 28.75 mi/s | 21.7 mi/s | 18.5 mi/s |
| Rotation period | 58 days, 15 hr | 243 days | 23 hr, 56 min |
| Sidereal period | 88 days | 224.7 days | 365.3 days |
| Diameter at equator | 3,030 mi | 7,520 mi | 7.926 mi |
| Mass (Earth's mass=1) | 0.06 | 0.8 | 1 |
| Surface temperature | 662F | 896 F | 72 F |
| Gravity (Earth's gravity =1) | 0.38 | 0.88 | 1 |
| Density (density of water =1) | 5.5 | 5.25 | 5.517 |
| Number of satellites known | 0 | 0 | 1 |
| Number of satellites known | 0 | 0 | 0 |

|                                 | **Mars**     | **Jupiter**  |
|---------------------------------|--------------|--------------|
| Mean distance from Sun          | 1.52 au      | 5.20 au      |
| Distance at perihelion          | 1.38 au      | 4.95 au      |
| Distance at aphelion            | 1.67 au      | 5.46 au      |
| Closest distance to Earth       | 0.38 au      | 3.95 au      |
| Average orbital speed           | 14.97 mi/s   | 8.14 mi/s    |
| Rotation period                 | 24 hr 37 min | 9 hr 50 min  |
| Sidereal period                 | 687 days     | 11.86 years  |
| Diameter at equator             | 4,222 mi     | 88,734 mi    |
| Mass (Earth's mass=1)           | 0.11         | 317.9        |
| Surface temperature             | -9 F         | -238 F       |
| Gravity (Earth's gravity =1)    | 0.38         | 2.64         |
| Density (density of water =1)   | 3.94         | 1.33         |
| Number of satellites known      | 2            | 16           |
| Number of rings known           | 0            | 1,000+       |

| Saturn | Uranus | Neptune | Pluto |
|--------|--------|---------|-------|
| 9.54 au | 19.18 au | 30.06 au | 39.36 au |
| 9.01 au | 18.28 au | 29.80 au | 29.58 au |
| 10.07 au | 20.09 au | 30.32 au | 49.14 au |
| 8.01au | 17.28 au | 28.80 au | 28.72 au |
| 5.97 mi/s | 4.23 mi/s | 3.36 mi/s | 2.92 mi/s |
| 10 hr 14 min | 16 hr 10 min | 18 hr 26 min | 6 days 9 hr |
| 29.46 yrs | 84.01 yrs | 164.8 yrs | 247.7 yrs |
| 74.566 mi | 31,566 mi | 30.137 mi | 3.725 mi |
| 95.2 | 14.6 | 17.2 | .002-0.003 |
| -2926F | -3460F | -364 F | -382 F |
| 1.15 | 1.17 | 1.2 | not known |
| 0.71 | 1.7 | 1.77 | not known |
| 19 | 5 | 2 | 1 |
| 9 | 0 | 0 | |

## The Sun

The Sun is estimated to be 4.5 billion years old. Since its birth it has used up about half of the hydrogen in its core. It will continue to radiate for another 5 billion years. Eventually, scientists are guessing that it will run out of hydrogen fuel.

At present, the Sun is a normal G2 star, one of more than 100 billion stars in our galaxy. Its most notable measurements are:

| | |
|---|---|
| **diameter:** | 1,390,000 km. |
| **mass:** | 1.989e30 kg |
| **temperature:** | 5800 K (surface) |
| | 15,600,000 K (core) |

The Sun is by far the largest object in the solar system. It contains more than 99.8% of the total mass of the Solar System, with Jupiter containing most of the rest. While there are many others similar to it in size, there are many more smaller stars than larger ones. The median size of stars in our galaxy is probably less than half the mass of the Sun.

Conditions at the Sun's core (approximately the inner 25% of its radius) are extreme. The temperature is 15.6 million Kelvin and the pressure is 250 billion atmospheres. At the center of the core the Sun's density is more than 150 times that of water. The surface of the Sun, called the photosphere, is at a temperature of about 5800 K. Sunspots are "cool" regions, only 3800 K (they only look dark by comparison to the surrounding regions). Sunspots can be very large, as much as 50,000 km in diameter. A small region known as the chromosphere lies above the photosphere. The highly rarefied region above the chromosphere, called the corona, extends millions of kilometers into space but is visible only during eclipses (left). Temperatures in the corona are over 1,000,000 K.

## The Moon

Earth's original satellite, the Moon, has guided people since ancient times. Scientists believe that the Moon was formed approximately the same time as the Sun, about 4.5 billion years ago. When the Moon formed, its outer layers melted under very high temperatures, forming the lunar crust, probably from a global "magma ocean."

The Moon is the fifth largest in the whole solar system. It rotates just once on its own axis in nearly the same time that it travels once around Earth. This is known as "synchronous rotation."

The Moon's surface is charcoal gray and sandy. This powdery blanket is called the lunar regolith, a term for mechanically produced debris layers on planetary surfaces. The regolith is thin. The interior of the Moon is made up of different layers of rock, some solid and some molten like lava.

## MOON UNITS

| | |
|---:|:---|
| **Distance from the Earth:** | 384,401 km |
| **Radius:** | 1737.4 km |
| **Mass:** | 7.3483 ◊ 1025 g |
| **Density:** | 3.341 g/cm3 |
| **Surface Gravity:** | 162.2 cm/s2 |
| **Rotational Period:** | Synchronous |
| **Orbital Period:** | 27.322 days |
| **Mean Orbit Velocity:** | 1.023 km/s |
| **Mean Surface Temperature:** | 107∞ C (day), |
| | -153∞ C (night) |